# BLACKPOOL'S
## Seaside Stars

The Gazette

# BLACKPOOL'S
# Seaside Stars

**Steve Singleton**                    **Craig Fleming**

DB
PUBLISHING

First published in Great Britain in 2009 by The Breedon Books Publishing Company Limited, Breedon House, 3 The Parker Centre, Derby, DE21 4SZ. ISBN 978-1-85983-741-2

Paperback edition published in Great Britain in 2012 by The Derby Books Publishing Company Limited, 3 The Parker Centre, Derby, DE21 4SZ.

ISBN 978-1-78091-118-2
Printed and bound by CPI Group (UK) Ltd, Croydon, CR0 4YY

# Contents

# Acknowledgements

A BOOK of this sort can only be researched, compiled and written with the co-operation of many people. Particular thanks go to the generations of *Gazette* photographers who captured these Seaside Stars both at work and at play over the decades, to *Gazette* chief librarian Carole Davies for hours of painstaking searching through the archives, with assistance from Mark Borland from the photographic department. In addition, thanks go to Blackpool entertainment historians Barry Band and Ken Shenton for their invaluable expert knowledge, to the Grand Theatre, Leisure Parks and to *Gazette* readers for their own memories.

# Introduction

**O**H WE do like to be beside the seaside…A timeless refrain not just from millions of Blackpool holidaymakers, but also from a galaxy of stars – who helped build the Lancashire resort's reputation as THE major entertainment centre outside London.

It was the northern mill workers who helped make Blackpool into Britain's number one holiday resort. They came in their droves to sample its unique atmosphere and bracing sea breezes.

They loved the Tower, the Golden Mile, the Illuminations and Piers, but they also demanded to be entertained throughout the decades.

The thirties saw the start of a golden era, with Blackpool beginning to gleam as the capital of seaside fun.

Stars of music hall, stage and screen – from both sides of the Atlantic – clamoured to perform in the resort, which could boast some of the biggest and best provincial theatres.

Even during the war years Blackpool was fondly regarded as a safe haven, which kept a smile on the face of thousands of service personnel and civil servants, dazzled by appearances by the country's top acts.

When the hostilities finally ended, Blackpool bounced back with the finest entertainments line-up in the country, in its heyday offering as many as 15 live shows each night during the summer season.

Just about every group and solo star of note in Britain and even America headed here during the fifties and sixties – live radio and TV specials came direct the resort which really knew how to rock.

The fun has continued since the seventies with families flocking to see summer season shows.

So step back in time with legends such as Gracie Fields, Jimmy Clitheroe, George Formby, Laurel and Hardy, Marlene Dietrich, Bob Hope, Hylda Baker, Thora Hird, Sid James, and even The Beatles.

More recent household names include Morecambe and Wise, Tommy Steele, Les Dawson, Bruce Forsyth, Russ Abbot, Ken Dodd and Cannon and Ball.

All have featured in Seaside Stars, a weekly feature within the *Gazette's* Memory Lane pages, that has proved such a hit that it has provided the basis for this book – a fascinating collection of celebrity profiles, together with many rare pictures from the archives, and sprinkled with *Gazette* readers' memories.

This selection only scratches the surface of Blackpool's remarkably deep and rich entertainment heritage, but we hope it will be a lasting souvenir to rekindle memories for residents and holidaymakers alike.

*Steve Singleton*

# Russ Abbot

CABBAGE Patch Kids accompanied TV funny man Russ Abbot when he met his fans on North Pier at the start of his record-breaking 1986 season show. His first solo season had been at the same theatre three years earlier, and he later returned in 1989 and 1992. But he had been a favourite with Blackpool audiences since 1976, when he appeared on South Pier as drummer with his showband, Opportunity Knocks winners the Black Abbots.

Russ went solo in 1980, and with his gallery of Madhouse characters – from airman Basildon Bond to Scottish loudmouth C U Jimmy – had high TV ratings.

Russ Abbot and the Cabbage Patch Kids at North Pier in 1986.

With furry friends at the Opera House, Blackpool, in 2000.

The entertainer showed his acting skills in the UK premiere of *Goosebumps* in 1999 and, the following year, in the title role of *Doctor Dolittle*, both at the Opera House.

Russ Abbot struggles with a deckchair on North Pier in 1986.

# Arthur Askey

**B**IG-HEARTED Arthur Askey always regarded a trip to Blackpool as a 'coming home'. The pint-sized entertainer, who found fame with silly songs like *The Busy Bee* and catchphrases like 'Hello Playmates' and 'Aythangyew', was probably Britain's best-loved comedian when he died.

The resort's staunchest supporter said of Blackpool in 1966, 'As far as seasons go, you can't touch Blackpool. I just love the Grand. Such a nice old fashioned theatre. It matches me.'

Arthur Bowden Askey was born in Liverpool on 6 June 1900. He did his first show in Blackpool, at the Tower, in 1939 and in the years following he played summer seasons at the Grand Theatre, Opera House and Palace Theatre, and appeared at the Tower Ballroom and ABC Theatre.

In his Blackpool Opera House dressing room in 1940 he achieved movie-star status when he signed an £83,000 contract to make five films at Shepherds Bush following the box office success of *Charley's (Big-Hearted) Aunt.*

Comedian Arthur Askey saying hello to playmates on Blackpool Promenade in 1953.

His wide range of work included radio, variety, pantomime and even comedy musical – starring opposite Thora Hird in the Grand Theatre's summer season farce *The Love Match* in 1953 – and he did three summer seasons there in other plays. Off stage, 5ft 2in Arthur loved cricket and golf down the road at St Annes Old Links.

Arthur's last Blackpool season was as a guest star in a Val Doonican show at the Opera House in 1969, during which he received word of his OBE. In typical Blackpool style, showbiz friends arranged a surprise party in the Winter Gardens Baronial Hall to pay tribute to the man they so deeply respected. The 200-strong guest list included Cilla Black, Roy Castle, Sid James, Reginald Dixon, Violet Carson, Moira Anderson, John Hanson, Mrs Mills and Jimmy Clitheroe.

Arthur gets down to some hard graft outside his Blackpool seafront hotel in 1966.

At the Buckingham Palace investiture, the Queen was reported as saying, 'This has been a long time coming'. Afterwards the personal aircraft of Charles Forte flew Arthur straight back to Blackpool.

In 1980 Arthur was due to host the BBC talent show *Rising Stars*, filmed at the ABC Theatre, but sadly he was forced to bow out because of an attack of shingles. He continued to suffer ill health and had both legs amputated before his death in November 1982.

*Memories*

'I saw The Love Match, *starring Arthur Askey, in 1953 at the Grand Theatre to celebrate my engagement to my wife to be, Lois, on her 21st birthday. Her father had organised a big party to celebrate her birthday but this was our celebration and we loved every minute of it.'*
*Ronald Mattock, Blackpool*

'*I remember seeing Arthur Askey at Coventry Hippodrome in the late thirties, with his grandma, when he was a boy. Thirty years later I was manager of Black's Mens Outfitters, opposite the Winter Gardens, and had a standing joke with Arthur that I could never sell him a shirt, as his collar size was 13in – youth. But I sold him many bow ties, socks, handkerchiefs and cufflinks. The memory I have of this big-hearted man is that he would always stop and wave to myself and staff when passing the door on his way to the Grand Theatre.'*
*John Mansfield, South Shore*

'*Arthur Askey and I were good friends and I worked with him on many occasions. He was charming and very kind. I first worked with him in Goody Two Shoes in Bournemouth in the fifties. He was an excellent Dame and I was just starting out in the business. He gave me so much good advice which helped my career enormously. Arthur had many problems but always kept a happy disposition. Even when in hospital – when he had his first leg amputated and was told he would have to lose the other – he said, "All my friends will think I'm leaving this world bit by bit!"'*
*Steve King, Thornton*

# Winifred Atwell

IT WAS undoubtedly the most decrepit piano in showbusiness. Pictured here with its owner Winifred Atwell on Central Pier, the battered piano, bought for 30 shillings in a council sale in London in 1951, was insured for £10,000. Winnie said 'It has an

Winifred Atwell at Central Pier in 1966.

Winifred Atwell in the kitchen of the Blackpool house she rented for the 1970 summer season in Carlin Gate, North Shore.

old iron frame, otherwise it wouldn't have stood up to all the travelling.'

So what about those carvings?

They began when a close friend carved his initials on the top right-hand side and after that it just snowballed.

'Stars who I have appeared with, theatre managers, friends and fans have carved their names or initials on the piano. I think there are about 4,000 names now.'

During its travels, the piano was taken down a mine, went aboard a submarine and was even on an airline's inaugural flight to New York.

The piano was never knowingly tuned – in fact Winnie de-tuned it to keep that well-known jangle effect. It was revealed, during a *Gazette* interview, that the piano was accidentally tuned at Blackpool's Hippodrome – where she played summer seasons in 1953 and 1958 – when a technician was called to the grand piano.

Winifred recalled, 'I had no idea until I sat down to play at the first house. I don't know who was more surprised, the audience or me!'

A qualified pharmacist from Trinidad, Winifred's first Blackpool appearance was at The Palace in 1949 when the *Gazette* declared her 'a Red Hot Momma of the piano'. Her last visit was in 1974 at the Opera House on her 25th anniversary tour and she had a summer season four years earlier at the Queen's Theatre.

# The Bachelors

**T**HREE-man harmony act The Bachelors performed their first summer season in 1964 on Central Pier, supporting comedian Al Read, just three months after their chart-topping success with *Diane*. The Irish entertainers – Dublin brothers Con and Dec Cluskey and friend John Stokes – were back two years later joining Cilla Black at the ABC Theatre.

Sunday concerts followed at the Opera House in 1967, where The Bachelors also did a full summer season in 1970, returning to the ABC in 1978 and Central Pier in 1983.

Following a split in the ranks, brothers Con and Dec, performing as The New Bachelors, were in summer shows on North Pier in 1987 and South Pier in 1994.

John Stokes, whose own version of The Bachelors has become a firm Blackpool favourite in recent years – including 1997 and 1998 North Pier runs – was back on stage in a Blackpool Seaside Special at the Winter Gardens Pavilion in 2008.

The Bachelors with Blackpool singer Helen Jayne in 1983.

The Bachelors in Blackpool for their show at the ABC in 1978.

# Hylda Baker

**S**HE MAY have been small in stature, but Hylda Baker was a bold and brassy comedy giant who loved life on the Fylde Coast. In a career spanning more than 60 years, Hylda remained fiercely proud of her Lancashire lass image and appeared in no fewer than eight Blackpool summer shows.

Born in Farnworth, near Bolton, she first went on stage at the age of 11 and spent many years in variety.

The diminutive dynamo's big TV break came – at the age of 50 – in April 1955 when she introduced Cynthia, a silent blonde – who was in fact a tall man in drag – and her famous catchphrase 'She knows y'now'.

That summer some 32 members of Hylda's family made the trip to the seaside to see her at the Queen's Theatre in Blackpool. They filled a

Hylda Baker outside her Squires Gate Holiday Camp chalet home, with pet monkeys Mickey and Coco, in 1955.

Hylda kicks-off a charity football match at Stanley Park, Blackpool, in 1970.

coach for the day out and visited Hylda at her caravan home at Squires Gate Holiday Camp in the afternoon.

When stage and TV stardom finally arrived, Hylda gained a reputation for big cars and luxury homes. She lived for many years at a handsome 11-bedroomed property called West Point, which had a commanding view of the Cleveleys promenade, furnishing it with her usual lack of taste.

She poured thousands into her home and even flew a blue and gold pennant carrying her famous catchphrase from a flagpole in the middle of her lawn. This pennant also adorned the sides of her huge black and gold American car, which she proudly drove up and down the Golden Mile as she took her two pet monkeys out for exercise.

She bought them after suffering a car crash. 'They were good for my nerves and made me laugh,' said Hylda, who dressed the pair of Brazilian Capuchin monkeys, called Mickey and Coco, in little jackets. Later she was said to have been inseparable from her Mexican Chihuahua dog Cha Cha, which she kept in her dressing room for many years.

It was with great sadness that Hylda later made the move to London because of work commitments. Her hilarious malapropisms saw her

Hylda Baker was a VIP guest at the Lytham Club Day festival in 1956.

become a household name in the TV sitcoms *Nearest and Dearest* and *Not on Your Nellie*. A stage version of *Nearest and Dearest*, which also starred Jimmy Jewel, played to a record-breaking 250,000 at the Grand Theatre in the summer of 1970, a record which saw her invited back to the theatre in 1977 to introduce the first bingo sessions. The following year she topped the bill in two concerts at the ABC Theatre, which were later featured in a BBC *Omnibus* programme.

At the age of 73, Hylda spent nine weeks at the top of the singles charts, with *You're The One That I Want* with Arthur Mullard, which sold 50,000 copies.

In later life Hylda suffered from Alzheimer's disease and she died at an actors' retirement home in Twickenham in 1986, aged 81.

# Derek Batey

**H**E HAS let thousands of couples share what they know about each other with everyone else and also made a fair number of them realise they didn't know so much after all!

We're talking about TV quiz show *Mr and Mrs*, which made a household name of Derek Batey, although he has always stressed that the couples are the real stars of the show and his maxim is to laugh with people, never at them. Derek, who was born in Brampton, near Carlisle, has lived in St Annes for 22 years.

Off screen, he reckons he has hosted the stage spin-off version of *Mr and Mrs* more than 800 times in Blackpool alone. It started in 1975 with an 11-year run on Central Pier, with two shows every Sunday. One summer a record was set, with Derek working on all three piers, adding in an early season of Saturdays on South and an Illuminations run on North. This meant that the stage set had to be packed up and moved up and down the Prom several times a week.

Other venues have included the Grand Theatre, Pleasure Beach Horseshoe Bar, Coral Island and a seven-year weekday season at Pontin's, Squires Gate.

Derek Batey presented a *Mr and Mrs* Blackpool Centenary contest at the Opera House in 1976 – pictured are winners Dorothy and Harold Leese.

Derek Batey with John Inman at a seafood stall on Central Pier in 1984.

# The Beatles

**B**EATLEMANIA swept Blackpool in the swinging sixties. For seven Sundays in the peak summer season of 1963 the Beatles were top of the pops and the resort was invaded by thousands of screaming fans.

The ABC chain booked a package of shows for the Blackpool ABC, where a fresh-faced Cliff Richard was starring with the Shadows for the summer. The deal included five Beatles concerts, and the mop-haired Merseysiders then had two vacant Sundays, which were eagerly snapped up by the Queen's Theatre. Central Pier producer Peter Webster had seen the lads play at the Marine Hall in Fleetwood in the summer of 1962 and had been offered the band for the 1963 season, but turned them down, later saying, 'I didn't think much of them.'

The Beatles returned in 1964 after conquering America. John, Paul, George and Ringo did a live telecast for ITV's *Blackpool Night Out* at the ABC on Sunday 19 July.

'What a scream,' the *Gazette* headline reported. All police leave was cancelled to cope with the crowds.

We loved them yeah, yeah, yeah – The Beatles during their 1964 visit to Blackpool.

The Beatles headlined two Sundays at the Opera House for promoter Harold Fielding. The first saw them mobbed as news leaked of their arrival and thousands of fans crowded the airport and town centre. The second was a softly-softly affair as the Beatles' arrival was kept a closely guarded secret.

A *Gazette* writer noted that they sang 10 songs that were barely heard for the screaming, which was said to reach its pitch when Ringo was singing *I Want To Be Your Man* on a darkened stage – while Paul's invitation to 'sort of clap your hands and sort of stamp your feet' got an 'ear-shattering response.'

The Beatles entered and left the Winter Gardens through the back door via the ballroom for their 26 July date where – 48 hours earlier – the Rolling Stones had been chased from the stage.

The Stones sparked a riot, amid 4,000 people, at the Empress Ballroom, when, according to local folklore, Keith Richards retaliated to a Scottish heckler. At the time Richards told the *Gazette*, 'A group of youths kept spitting at us while we were playing. I lost my temper and tried to kick him. He just went too far.'

Mick Jagger added, 'These lads wouldn't stop it and Keith lost his temper. I suppose he shouldn't have done it.'

Emotions ran high. Tables, chairs and mirrors were smashed. The Stones fled...smuggled out of the building by a rooftop exit.

The Beatles were back for another of their Blackpool TV shows at the ABC in August 1965, which included the first public performance of *Yesterday* by Paul McCartney. He sang the world's most recorded song solo to the backing of his own acoustic guitar.

The Beatles on the stage of the ABC Theatre, the venue for their live Sunday night TV concerts, which included the debut of *Yesterday* by Paul McCartney in August 1965.

# Cilla Black

**I**T MIGHT be a 'Surprise Surprise' to younger readers, but there was a time when Blackpool had a host of summer shows – and the theatres to hold them – each packing two houses a night.

That was certainly still the case in 1969 when former Liverpool typist Cilla Black was enjoying the second of her three seasons – *Holiday Startime* at the ABC.

Cilla's first resort appearance was at the Queen's Theatre on Easter Sunday 1964, three weeks after her chart-topping success with *Anyone Who Had A Heart*. She returned that August for a live telecast of *Blackpool Night Out* at the ABC. Her last season show was at the Opera House in 1972, although she did return for Sunday variety concerts at the ABC in June and July 1973 and North Pier in 1982.

The final line up of Miss UK 1969 (at Blackpool Open Baths), featuring judges Val Doonican, Sid James and Cilla Black.

Cilla Black at a St Annes Civil Service garden party in 1969.

# Charlie Cairoli

CHARLIE CAIROLI was Blackpool's clown prince for nearly 40 years. With his world-famous red nose, white make-up and trademark bowler hat, his was the face that stopped countless custard pies and made young and old alike laugh until they wept.

A member of a four-generation circus family, sawdust was in Charlie's veins when he came to Blackpool Tower Circus in 1939. His mother was a trapeze artiste and juggler and his father was a clown with his own enviable reputation. He learned his trade the hard way and, by the time he reached his teens, he had appeared as an acrobat, horse rider, conjurer and musician.

As the *Gazette's* own HRG said, 'I remember his first appearance in the summer of 1939. He was irresistible with his sophisticated slapstick, his musical skill and his sheer professional expertise. War clouds were darkening the landscape, but Charlie lightened them. He loved the laughter of children. He would have brushed aside any notion that he

Charlie Cairoli at the Tower Circus with sidekick Paul in 1958.

A mesmerising meeting with Charlie Cairoli for this little girl in 1976.

followed the steps of one who suffered little children to come to him, and made them happy. But he did just that.'

As the accolades came in after the war, he became 'Uncle Charlie of Blackpool' and was billed as 'clown prince of laughter' and 'one of the world's greatest clowns' – and few would disagree.

With his unique blend of French and Lancashire accents, Charlie, who made his home in Blackpool's North Shore, was the last of the classic clowns whose seemingly effortless foolery went into three Tower shows a day, every summer. He also appeared in pantomime and Christmas circuses in London and starred in his own children's BBC TV programme, *Right Charlie*, for 10 years.

In the summer of 1979 Charlie was ordered to quit by chest specialists after missing some 12 weeks of the circus – his first absence during his long association with the Tower. Sadly he died in February 1980, aged 70 – less than three months after announcing his retirement from circus life.

# ⋅⋆⋆⋆ Cannon and Ball ⋆⋆⋆⋅⋆⋅

**A**T THE height of their popularity, comedy double act Cannon and Ball played to more than one million people during their 1985 summer season, UK tour and panto. And the star duo certainly conquered Blackpool in 1980, with a record-breaking North Pier summer season.

The duo were former workmates in a Lancashire engineering factory in the early 1960s. By day they were welders Robert Harper and Tommy Derbyshire, but by night they became a singing duo called The Harper Brothers.

It soon became evident that Bobby had a natural flair for comedy, with Tommy the perfect straight-faced foil. As the comedy content grew stronger, so did their popularity, and the name change, four years after they started out, certainly helped.

Cannon and Ball with vote for fun rosettes outside the Winter Gardens in 1987.

Lighting the fuse for the 1980 Blackpool Illuminations switch-on.

Cannon and Ball launch their showbusiness silver anniversary on North Pier in 1991.

The duo's first TV appearance was in 1972 in the variety show *The Wheeltappers and Shunters Social Club* and stardom quickly followed.

*The Cannon and Ball Show* was first shown in 1979 and further series were screened each year until 1988, along with top TV-rating Christmas and Easter specials.

The boys were back as top billing in Blackpool with summer seasons at the Opera House in 1985 and 1987.

By the 1990s the duo were seeking a change in direction and appeared in their own sitcom *Cannon and Ball's Playhouse*, the spin-off series *Plaza Patrol* and their game show *Cannon and Ball's Casino*.

However, they remained loyal to their Lancashire roots and starred at the North Pier in 1991 and the Opera House again in 1994. Two years later they headlined a *Rock With Laughter* season at the Grand Theatre.

Blackpool had certainly become their second home, and in 1999 they returned to headline the Grand's summer show *Comedy Bonanza*, a formula repeated in 2002, 2004 and 2005. Family man Bobby in fact made the move to nearby St Annes.

In more recent times they have continued to find success as a comic duo in theatre and pantomime, along with numerous cameo appearances on TV. The pair also revived a touring version of the theatrical farce *Big Bad Mouse*, originally a highly successful vehicle for Jimmy Edwards and Eric Sykes in the 1960s and 1970s.

# Frank Carson

'IT'S THE way he tells them' – that is why loveable Frank Carson has been a Blackpool summer-season favourite since the seventies. The Belfast-born comic's famous catchphrase was in fact coined at a club in Colne, Lancashire, in 1968. 'There was a man in the front row who was the only person in the audience not laughing,' said Frank.

'Then after one joke he laughed and when I asked what he liked about that particular one he just said it was the way I told it.'

After that Frank began to use the phrase in his quick-fire act until it became his trademark.

'I don't know who the man was but I must owe him millions.'

'But it isn't really the way I tell them at all,' he admitted. 'It's the way I laugh when I'm telling them. Someone can tell me a joke and I can make them laugh by telling it back to them in my own style.'

Frank first found fame as an outright winner on Hughie Green's *Opportunity Knocks*, and then starred in *The Good Old Days*. Today he

Frank Carson on North Pier, Blackpool, where he headlined the 1997 summer show.

Frank Carson with his good friend and
golfing pal Les Dawson in 1982.

Motormouth Irish comedian Frank Carson, pictured here in 1983, made his home on the Fylde Coast.

has a lifetime of Blackpool memories. His Blackpool season shows began at the North Pier in 1972 with the stage spin-off of *The Comedians*.

A proud resident of Blackpool for more than 20 years, he went on to star in the *All Laughter Showtime* at the North Pier for the summer of 1977 and *The All Laughter Spectacular* at the Opera House in 1979. In 1988 he was back at the Opera House, followed by three seasons at the South Pier in the early nineties.

In 1997, aged 71, he celebrated 50 years in showbusiness and showed no signs of slowing down with a spring season at the North Pier.

The summer of 1998 was spent at the Central Pier and the following year he starred in *Comedy Bonanza* at the Grand Theatre.

# Roy Castle

**E**NTERTAINER Roy Castle was known as the Mr Nice Guy of showbusiness, and his courageous fight against cancer touched millions of hearts. A song and dance man, Roy grew up in Cleveleys and always had a love for the Fylde.

Roy Castle with Cilla Black in Blackpool in 1969.

In November 1958 the *Gazette* reported that Cleveleys was proud of its new star, 26-year-old Roy Castle, who had come to 'overnight fame' in the *Royal Variety Show* – nine years after he had made his debut in the town.

'His sensational success, which swept a comparative unknown to stardom, is today the talking point in the district which has seen him grow up from his early days in the summer season show *Happiness Ahead* at the Queen's Theatre, Cleveleys, to his present position.'

Singer, dancer, entertainer, Roy Castle, aged 14.

Roy Castle enjoys some cricket fun with his young family in 1969.

In March 1956 Huddersfield-born Roy was on a touring variety bill that stopped off at Blackpool's Queen's Theatre, where that summer he was signed up to appear with Jimmy James' *Lets Have Fun on Central Pier*.

Just four weeks before the *Royal Variety Show*, he had been third down the bill below singer Dickie Valentine and comic Norman Vaughan at Blackpool's Palace Theatre. In 1959 Roy was back there as one of the stars of its summer show.

As Roy became one of TV's most prolific entertainers, he starred in just one more Blackpool season show, with Cilla Black, at the ABC in 1969, although he returned for Grand Theatre concerts in the 1980s. He also found a new audience by carving out a reputation as the daredevil presenter of *Record Breakers* for more than 20 years, which included an abseil down Blackpool Tower.

In 1992 non-smoker Roy, hailed as the People's Hero, revealed he had lung cancer and he died in 1994, the day before he was due to have been an Illuminations switch-on guest, although his son Ben performed there – to a standing ovation – as a member of the National Youth Jazz Orchestra.

# ✦✦ Jimmy Clitheroe ✦✦✦

**P**INT-SIZED entertainer Jimmy Clitheroe, who made Blackpool his home, built a career out of the illusion of eternal youth. Yet many of his fans were surprised to learn that he was 51 when he died on the day of his mother's funeral in 1973.

Struck by the magic of the Tower Circus, which he visited from his East Lancashire home at the age of six, Jimmy's own Blackpool debut came in the mid-1930s in the juvenile team Winstanley's Babes at Feldman's Theatre.

The following decade he and his mother – to whom he was devoted – moved to Bispham Road, Bispham, and over the years the 4ft 3in eternal schoolboy became a great favourite of Blackpool holiday audiences, and he was also very successful in pantomime.

When Jimmy was out and about in Blackpool he created tales galore. Many people thought they were seeing a small boy at the wheel of a big car or drinking in pubs.

The face of the impish schoolboy, who was one of Britain's box-office stars, concealed a shrewd businessman. Jimmy had several business

Diminutive comic Jimmy Clitheroe helped Mayor Edmund Wynne open Blackpool Model Village in 1972.

Jimmy Clitheroe with a treat for a Blackpool donkey in 1959.

interests at various periods, including a Blackpool turf accountants and a country restaurant.

He appeared in 16 Blackpool season shows, including the Queen's, Central Pier, the Grand and Winter Gardens Pavilion.

As well as packing theatres for live appearances, Jimmy also enjoyed a 15-year radio run in 290 episodes of *The Clitheroe Kid* from 1957, which won him fans worldwide.

One of his proudest moments came in June 1960 when he was presented to the Queen Mother at a *Royal Variety Show* at the Palace Theatre, Manchester.

Jimmy Clitheroe.

Jimmy's last Blackpool summer season was at the Queen's Theatre, alongside Josef Locke, in 1971.

Jimmy was found unconscious in bed at his Bispham home on the day of his mother's funeral. The Blackpool coroner later recorded a verdict of 'accidental death' from the combined effects of sleeping pills and alcohol.

*Memories*

*'Jimmy Clitheroe and I used to play snooker together in the Squirrel pub. I was just a teenager in those days, but Jimmy always had time for the locals and life was never dull with him around. The abiding memory I have of Jimmy is him always having to use a rest to play his snooker shots!'*

*Bill Green, Blackpool*

# Jim Davidson

'**F**UN 4 U' claimed the number plate when controversial comedian Jim Davidson got behind the wheel in Blackpool for his first full headlining summer season in 1993.

It was at the Opera House, where he had previously enjoyed success with a series of 15 Sunday shows in 1991. Jim, 1976 winner of TV's *New Faces*, made his resort debut in the cast of the 1977 *All Laughter Showtime* on North Pier with Little and Large, Norman Collier and Frank Carson.

Other Blackpool offerings have included festive seasons at the Opera House with his adult panto *Sinderella* and *Stand-Up for Christmas*.

Jim Davidson was joined by veteran comic Charlie Drake for his adult panto *Sinderella* at the Opera House in 1996.

Jim Davidson at the wheel for his first headlining summer season at the Opera House in 1993.

# Bette Davis

'**B**LACKPOOL was one of my favourite memories of that first trip to England,' said Bette Davis when she met Mayor Harold Hoyle ahead of an appearance at the ABC Theatre in October 1975.

That first visit was in September 1936 and Bette stayed at the County Hotel, crossing the Promenade to be photographed and interviewed by the *Gazette*.

She checked in under her married name as Mrs H.O. Nelson, California. It was the answer to the question newspapers were asking on both sides of the Atlantic: Where is Bette Davis?

She had vanished from Hollywood after a row with film magnate Jack Warner, head of the mighty Warner Brothers organisation. Bette, reaching the peak of her career, felt her scripts were declining in quality and, after arguing with Warner, she was told she should take her new role – or else. It was as a female lumberjack in *God's Country and The Woman*, and Bette said 'I flatly refused to play it. The heroine was an insufferable bore who scowled while everyone kept yelling "timber".'

She was suspended for three months with no salary and later signed with another studio, ultimately sailing to England to avoid an injunction which would have prohibited her from working.

The Nelsons vanished from London and turned up in Blackpool, where the *Gazette* recorded that 'she emerged in the hotel lounge, charming and glamorous'.

A wave from Bette Davis on Blackpool Promenade in 1936.

# Les Dawson

T O MANY people Les Dawson was a legend and the Fylde's favourite funny man. Lugubrious Les adopted the Fylde as his home when stardom finally came his way. He became one of Lytham St Annes' most famous adopted sons in 1975 and an unstinting ambassador for Britain's top seaside resort until his untimely death, aged 60, in 1993.

When encouraged to take a well-earned foreign holiday, Les once joked 'If I go abroad I'll just get drunk on cheap plonk, baste in the sun and probably return home with the runs. I'll stick to Blackpool and Lytham St Annes. It's smashing – I love living here.'

Salford-born Les, who entertained millions with his spoof piano playing, gurning faces, eloquent tales and mother-in-law gags, made his first Blackpool appearance in 1964 – a week's cabaret at the Lobster Pot in Market Street.

Les will forever be remembered for his Cissie and Ada partnership with Roy Barraclough.

Les tees off in inimitable style for the 16th Les Dawson charity golf tournament at Fairhaven GC in May 1991.

Les at the piano as he tells another rib-tickling tale in January 1986.

Three years later the resort was to be a turning point for him when his droll comedy made an impact as a support act on ABC TV's live *Blackpool Night Out* variety show.

He was back a month later, in August 1967, and on the strength of that signed for a support spot on the 1968 Central Pier season show.

In 1971 Les shared the honours with Dora Bryan at the Queen's Theatre. His third Blackpool season was at the ABC in 1977, and in 1984 – the year he began his long run as host of BBC TV's *Blankety Blank* – he starred at the Grand Theatre, when highlights included his Cissie and Ada double act with Roy Barraclough (an act first seen at an Opera House Sunday concert three years earlier) and Les's 'discoveries', the Roly Polys.

Lancashire's own master of mirth was back at the Grand in 1986 with the summer farce *Run For Your Wife*, which returned in October 1987 for a month.

Unfortunately, *The Les Dawson Laughter Show* at the Opera House in 1988 was to be the comedian's sixth and final season, closing early because of his ill health.

A blue plaque, honouring one of the world's comedy legends, was mounted by Comic Heritage outside his Ansdell home in 1995 and a £60,000 statue of Les was unveiled in a new Garden of Fame, next to St Annes Pier, in October 2008.

# Marlene Dietrich

**H**USKY-VOICED Marlene Dietrich was one of the most famous women of her time when she came to Blackpool. The smouldering sex symbol, who hypnotised her public with her sultry half-talking, half-singing style, performed two sell-out concerts at the Opera House on Sunday 17 July 1955.

Fabulous is a word which is bandied about far too often these days, but this was a unique opportunity for 6,000 Blackpool theatregoers to see one of the true 'greats'.

For the German-born film star who firmly turned her back on Hitler's Nazis, it was a novel experience, as this was her only show away from the Café de Paris, one of London's most glittering and expensive nightspots. And besides being her only show outside London, it was also Dietrich's debut before a vast audience on a concert platform.

Although Marlene's visit was a flying one – arriving by a special charter plane during the afternoon – she still requested a tour of the resort to see Blackpool as the holidaymakers knew it.

On the night, the world's most glamorous grandmother, who in fact was aged 50, made her dramatic entrance to Gershwin's *Rhapsody in Blue*. There were gasps as the star of the 1930s *The Blue Angel* appeared. She wore a Snow Queen-like, slinky shimmering gown, her shoulders were swathed in white fur, and she sang the numbers which still entrance in that broken accent, including *Lili Marlene* and *Fallin In Love Again*.

The legend proved to be just that. She died in Paris aged 90 in 1992.

Marlene Dietrich requested a tour of Blackpool after flying into Squires Gate for her two shows in 1955.

Marlene Dietrich as she was seen at the Opera House in 1955.

*Memories*

'*I was in her audience in 1955. It brought tears to my eyes. Her appearance was the most memorable Opera House show that I ever saw.*'

*L. Booth, St Andrews Road, St Annes*

# Reginald Dixon

REGINALD DIXON earned worldwide acclaim for playing Blackpool Tower's mighty Wurlitzer organ. For most of his glittering 40-year career he was known to millions as Mr Blackpool.

A profoundly shy figure beneath the ebullience of his playing, his prowess earned him fans around the globe – with thousands of broadcasts which were relayed by the BBC throughout the Commonwealth. In particular his rendition of *I Do Like To Be Beside The Seaside* made him and Blackpool household names throughout the world.

Yorkshire-born Reg gave his first performance at the Tower at Easter 1930 and a successful career took him to Buckingham Palace in 1966 to receive the MBE. His records sold in many countries, including the United States and New Zealand.

Proud to claim the status of a naturalised Lancastrian, Dixon once said, 'To me, Blackpool is my home and there is an attraction about it which you can't get away from, though it's hard to define.'

A telegraph of congratulations from Bing Crosby was among the good wishes from all over the world received by Reginald Dixon before his farewell concert in 1970.

Dixon retired on reaching the age of 65 in Easter 1970, but music remained his first love and he then toured venues across Britain to perform on an electric organ. He died in 1985, aged 80.

Organist Reginald Dixon pictured at the Wurlitzer organ in the magnificent Tower Ballroom in 1958.

# Ken Dodd

**K**EN DODD is a comedy legend with few equals. Liverpool-born Ken, who was 81 in November 2008, has been delivering rib-tickling shows full of 'plumptiousness' for more than 50 laughter-filled years. And Doddy has shown no signs of slowing up! He travels up to 100,000 miles a year to 150 gigs to make sure that the nation's chuckle muscles are in full working order.

Ken Dodd and his Diddymen on Blackpool promenade in 1978.

'Hats off to Blackpool Magic', says Ken Dodd in 1991.

While most shows sell ice-creams and chocolate in the interval, at a Ken Dodd show there's the option to buy a sleeping bag, as he has a habit of running over time and finishing after midnight.

'A lot of men retire because they've had enough, but I'm still stage struck. I still love the one nights and there's always something new to experience. There's nothing quite like a good laugh for airing the lungs and exercising the chuckle muscles.'

Sir Harry Secombe chats to Ken Dodd on Blackpool's North Pier as part of a *Songs of Praise* recording in 1996.

Ken still loves every minute of his life in showbusiness and he has a soft spot for Blackpool and in particular the Grand Theatre, where he is a proud patron, having launched the Grand's centenary appeal in 1994.

'Blackpool has always been good to me. Kenneth Arthur Dodd may live in Knotty Ash, but Ken Dodd the performer's home is right here in Blackpool. I think I have done more seasons here than any other performer. This is the greatest show town in the world and Blackpool people are the greatest hosts in the world.'

Ken's love affair with Blackpool began when he was a little-known comic, billed as the The Laughter Lad, on the Central Pier's *Let's Have Fun* 1955 summer show, when the stars were Morecambe and Wise. He was an instant success, and returned for a second Pier season the following year, while in 1957 he topped the summer show bill at the Hippodrome in *Rocking with Laughter*.

His incredible appearance record includes six summer seasons at the Opera House from 1975, since when he has rarely missed a year. His total of thousands of summer shows and Sunday concerts at the Opera House and the Grand Theatre make him Blackpool's true comedy king.

# ·····✦✦ Val Doonican ✦✦✦·····

**W**ITH HIS rugged sweaters and clean-cut wholesome manner, you might imagine that Val Doonican would be at home beside the sea – but you would be wrong!

'I'm not a lover of the seaside. I never liked beaches even as a child,' said the genial Irishman, who nevertheless found himself contributing to Blackpool's entertainment heritage.

Val Doonican and his wife Lynn try out Blackpool's inshore lifeboat during his Opera House season in 1974.

Val Doonican opened the Fleetwood Sea Cadets annual summer fair in 1966.

TV's most relaxed singer, famed for his velvet voice and rocking chair, found himself starring in his first summer show at the old Queen's Theatre, Blackpool, in 1966.

'I used to nip out to see the "rich relations" up the road – The Bachelors at the ABC and Ken Dodd at the Opera House – and I remember thinking how fantastic it must be to walk out on to that big Opera House stage,' said Val, who brought his family to live in St Annes for the summer. From there he managed three mornings a week to get on to St Annes Old Links course, where he was a mean seven handicapper. Three years later Val found out he was the star of the Opera House's 1969 season show, supported by Moira Anderson and Arthur Askey.

Val returned to star in another Opera House season in 1974 and performed a series of Sunday concerts in the Opera House. He won many of the top honours in entertainment and appeared in three *Royal Variety Shows*.

One afternoon he deserted his rocking chair for something far more exciting – donning bright orange waterproofs with his wife Lynn for a 15-minute trip in the inshore lifeboat in choppy seas off Central Promenade.

His last Blackpool appearance was at the Grand Theatre in June 1994.

# Gracie Fields

SING as we go...the eternal Lancashire lass Gracie Fields had a life-long love affair with Blackpool. Her first visit was as a member of a poor children's outing from Rochdale. She was seven and got lost under North Pier just as the tide was coming in. At 14 she played the resort professionally, running away to the seaside in the hope of joining a juvenile troupe.

Gracie Fields at the top of Blackpool Tower in the 1950s.

Gracie Fields takes a donkey ride on Blackpool beach in 1927.

Gracie pictured in 1967 when she visited her beloved Blackpool to open the Brindle Lodge old people's centre on Mereside.

Gracie topped show bills in Blackpool in five different decades, starting at the old Palace Theatre in 1923 in her first husband Archie Pitt's long-running *Tower of London* revue.

All of her major 1920s revues were seen in Blackpool and, during her Grand Theatre variety performances the following decade, there were 14 weeks of sold-out shows from 1932 to 1938.

In 1964, 30 years after filming *Sing As We Go* in the resort, she finally achieved a life-long ambition to turn on the Illuminations, singing *Sally* and *Volare*, and later commenting, 'I only go to Capri for a bit of peace and quiet. I'd rather be in Blackpool.'

*Memories*

'*I worked in the Town Hall the night 'Our Gracie' switched on the Lights in 1964. She arrived at the side entrance of the Town Hall with the Mayor. Her Italian husband Boris seemed bewildered at the effect she had on the assembled guests as she was taken up the main staircase to the Mayor's Parlour. She seemed to know everyone as they shouted 'Hello Gracie Love'. It was as if she had entered her own home...Blackpool was hers and she knew it.*

*To me she looked like a very wealthy Blackpool landlady just back from a cruise. On her way out to the platform to pull the switch I was positioned in the main entrance guarding a giant stick of rock which would be presented to her after the switch on. She gave me one of those cheeky ladette winks which made me feel part of the show.*

*Later in the Parlour the Mayor presented her with a hostess trolley...a gift from the people of Blackpool. She said she would take it to Capri. Many years later I saw a television programme in her Capri home showing Gracie giving cups of tea to the many fans who made the pilgrimage to see her. I am almost certain I spotted the hostess trolley given by Blackpool.'*

*Barry Morris*

# Flanagan and Allen

**M**USIC HALL comedy greats Flanagan and Allen were frequent performers in Blackpool. Funny man Bud Flanagan, the son of a Polish Jew, was actually born in London and named Chaim Reeven (Reuben) Weintrop, and the story goes that he took his stage name during World War One from a sergeant-major he disliked, telling him, 'When the war is over, I shall use your name on stage, you horrible little man.'

He was teamed with straight man Chesney Allen in the mid-1920s, and the duo eventually found fame in the Crazy Gang. They performed 13 Command Performances before British monarchs, including the 1955 *Royal Variety Show* at Blackpool Opera House.

Even before the Crazy Gang existed – they were not founder members – Flanagan and Allen performed at The Palace, Blackpool, as part of Florrie Forde's variety company.

Blackpool was also pivotal in re-uniting the duo during World War Two, the partners being separated when the London Palladium closed its doors. They made a pact that in the event of separation they should reserve accommodation at the Clifton Hotel and wait for each other.

The *Gazette* carried news of Bud's arrival on 21 September 1940, and four days later they were reunited on the telephone after Allen was spotted on the south coast by a man who showed him a copy of the newspaper article.

The double act ended on Allen's retirement in 1945. Flanagan, who continued to perform, died aged 72 in 1968, outlived by Allen, who died in 1982, aged 89.

Bud Flanangan and Chesney Allen –
Blackpool was pivotal in re-uniting the duo
during World War Two.

# ✷✷ George Formby ✷✷✷

**T**URNED out nice again...seven times over, in fact, for comedy king George Formby in Blackpool. That is the number of season shows – four of them at the Opera House – in which George thrilled fans during his 30 years at the top, and it would surely have been a lot more seaside appearances but for his non-stop output of films and hit records.

The unpretentious Wigan-born clown with the wide, toothy grin became Britain's highest-paid comedian and most popular film star of the thirties.

He played to audiences all over the world, before the Royal Family, and before millions of fans.

His first small supporting appearance had been at the Palace Theatre in June 1923, progressing upwards through the showbills with the help and guidance of his wife Beryl.

George Formby switches on the Blackpool Illuminations in 1953.

A galloping George Formby on the beach in 1950.

Star of stage and screen George Formby made his home on the Fylde.

He made his first film in 1932 and scores of comedies followed. In 1933 George was resident host for Jack Taylor's *Variety Fair* at the Palace, his first Blackpool season, followed by *King Fun* at the Opera House in 1936 and *King Cheer* in 1937.

Look who's cleaning windows – George Formby with his Rolls-Royce and Jaguar cars and their distinctive number plates outside his St Annes home in 1958.

Growing movie fame made banjulele-playing George the obvious choice to open the new Opera House for the 1939 season with *Turned Out Nice Again*. He was also to star in the 1946 show there, *Starry Way*.

He became ill during the 1954 Hippodrome summer season, but was well enough to appear in the following year's *Royal Variety Show* at the Opera House. His final Blackpool season was at the Queen's Theatre in 1960.

George made his home in the Fylde – at Little Singleton, Barton and Barnacre – before a final move to Beryldene on St Annes promenade.

Always a keen motorist, his 'stable' included Rolls-Royces and Jaguars. His other love was his yacht *Lady Beryl*.

Beryl died on Christmas Day 1960, ending a partnership that had begun in 1924. In February 1961 he announced his engagement to 36-year-old school teacher Pat Howson from Penwortham, but he died the following month, aged 56, after a history of heart problems.

# Bruce Forsyth

**B**RUCE FORSYTH was a one-time bill-topper in Blackpool. While these days he is thought of as one of TV's long-time favourite game show hosts, and more recently presenter of BBC's *Strictly Come Dancing*, there was always much more to his talent than just a catchphrase or two.

The song and dance man first appeared in Blackpool in 1946 when he played with Jack Jackson's Band at the Palace Theatre. In the late 1950s he found TV stardom with *Sunday Night at the London Palladium*, coining the catchphrase 'I'm in charge' as volunteers tried to *Beat The Clock*. In 1960 he was in charge of his own summer season show, Bernard Delfont's *Show Time* at the North Pier Pavilion, and he was seldom off the stage.

He earned this accolade from a *Gazette* reviewer: 'This great personality with his long jaw and even greater endowment of cheek has a rare gift for making people enjoy themselves.'

Bruce Forsyth at the opening of Carley's fashion shop in Birley Street, Blackpool, in 1959.

Bruce Forsyth has trouble with his deckchair in Blackpool in 1960.

Bruce Forsyth in golfing action at Royal Lytham in 1967.

Also in the show was his Irish-born wife, under her stage name Penny Calvert, who proved a versatile singer and dancer. They had two children, Deborah and Julie, and rented a home in South Shore for the season. The couple divorced in 1968.

Bruce returned to the resort to star in the summer season show at the Opera House in 1967, alongside Millicent Martin, and brought his own one-man show to the Opera House on Easter Monday 1975. His last visit was *An Evening with Bruce Forsyth* at the Grand Theatre in June 1988.

Away from the stage there were a few whirlwind visits. One saw him at Weeton Army Camp making a TV advert about that margarine 'which can be spread with nothing on' alongside Poulton Girl Guides in December 1976.

*Memories*

'*I recall watching Bruce Forsyth at the Opera House in 1967. My wife and I, and our two children, were sat four rows back in the centre front stalls. The orchestra struck up the opening bars of the* National Anthem, *but as I knew this was part of the act I told the family to stay seated. Brucie looked down and said, 'You'll stand up before the end.' At the end of the show, and after the customary* National Anthem *finished, Bruce appeared from behind the curtain, looked at me, and said, "Told you so!"'*
D.C. Parsons

'*I remember Bruce visiting the resort. He opened Carley's new fashion shop in Birley Street, Blackpool, in November 1959 and he opened Collins Trademarket at Marton in April 1977.*'
Harry Smith, Bond Street, South Shore

# ⋆✦✦ Freddie Frinton ✦✦✦

**F**REDDIE FRINTON, seen here with co-star Thora Hird in one of their two Grand Theatre seasons together, was also well-known for *Dinner For One* – his classic drunken sketch, performed in three Blackpool summer shows.

He always took the role of an elderly butler at a five-course dinner at which he asked the dowager Miss Sophie, 'Same procedure as last year Miss Sophie?' To which the old dear would reply, 'Same procedure as every year, James.'

Freddie Frinton at the Grand Theatre in 1965 with Thora Hird in *My Perfect Husband*.

Freddie would then voice and drink the toasts to the invisible guests, getting progressively more drunk.

At the end of the sketch – but this time with a look of dread – he would again ask, 'Same procedure as last year Miss Sophie?' and she would reply, 'Same procedure as every year, James.'

And the couple would walk off stage arm in arm, leaving the rest to the imagination.

Freddie appeared at the Winter Gardens Pavilion in 1954, and the Opera House in 1956 and 1960, although his first visit had been to the Palace in 1949.

The two Grand summer plays with Thora Hird were *The Best Laid Schemes* in 1962 and, pictured on the previous page, *The Perfect Husband*.

At short notice, Freddie unexpectedly starred in his third Grand summer offering, *Wedding Fever*, in 1967, stepping in for Sid James, who was taken ill.

*Memories*

'*Freddie's single act comedy* Dinner For One *caught the attention of a German TV producer who recorded it for German television in 1963. The play was recorded in English in front of a German TV audience and has now become part of German folklore. It has been repeated every New Year's Eve since 1972. The show clocks up 15 or so repeats every year, making Herr Frinton's* Dinner For One *one of the most repeated TV programmes in the world.'*
*Paul Breeze, of South Shore*

# ✦✦ Judy Garland ✦✦

**B**LACKPOOL scored a major coup when Judy Garland came to the resort. The big-screen superstar appeared in front of more than 6,000 people in two shows at the Opera House. Fans waited outside the stage door and crowded around the theatre for a glimpse of the 28-year-old star on Sunday 24 June 1951.

On stage, the *Gazette* reviewer noted that Judy was somewhat plumper than the wide-eyed girl who had enchanted us all in *The Wizard of Oz*. Nevertheless, she enthralled two packed houses, during which she mopped her brow and asked leave to take off her high-heeled shoes 'as she could sing better without them'.

At curtain close, as she clasped a bouquet, she expressed the hope that Blackpool would one day invite her back. Although she later made further British tours, sadly her return visit never happened.

Judy Garland before her two shows at the Opera House in 1951.

# John Gielgud

COULD you imagine Macbeth as an Easter attraction in Blackpool? Well, it happened in 1942 when hundreds of relocated war-weary civil servants and thousands of RAF personnel needed entertainment – and headed for the Opera House.

It was John Gielgud's third appearance in the resort in less than four years, and the *Gazette* reported, 'Mr Gielgud not only played Macbeth with fine art, understanding and balance, but his genius was evident as producer – a memorable evening.'

The first of the Gielgud visits was for a week at the Grand Theatre in 1939 in his own production of Oscar Wilde's *The Importance of Being Earnest*. The cast included Edith Evans, Peggy Ashcroft, Margaret Rutherford and Jack Hawkins.

Two years later Gielgud was back at the Grand in J.M. Barrie's *Dear Brutus*.

Born in 1904, the actor, who was knighted in 1953, died in 2000.

Sir John Gielgud, who made three visits to Blackpool.

# Terry Hall

**V**ENTRILOQUIST Terry Hall created his famous companion in Blackpool. So rather than a sand grown'un you could almost call Lenny the Lion a grand sewn'un!

The hapless cat came to life from a bundle of fox fur, papier mâché and a golf ball for a nose after Terry, a popular act at many of Blackpool's long-demolished theatres, visited the Tower Zoo in the early 1950s.

Terry was moderately successful with his dummy Mickey Flynn, with whom he had made his first Blackpool appearance in variety at the Palace Theatre in January 1948, but he realised he needed a new character in order to achieve broader recognition and Lenny was brought to life by props maker Fred Drummond in his Squires Gate workshop.

Once the doll was ready, all that was missing was a name. This was suggested by his co-star Anne Shelton. Lenny thus gained a falsetto, lisping tone and achieved stardom for himself and Terry.

Terry Hall with Lenny the Lion and fellow stars of Blackpool Queen's Theatre season show in 1957.

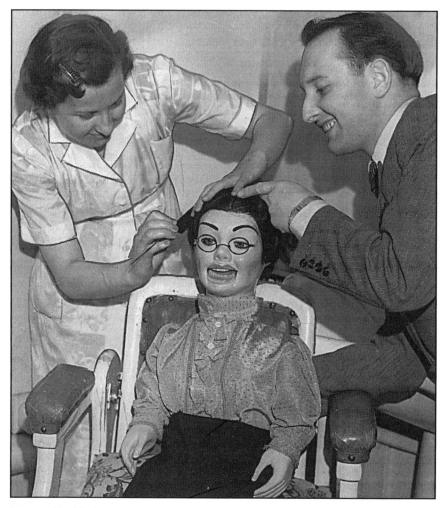

Terry Hall with dummy Winnie Winterbottom and hairdresser Betty Yardley before a performance of *On With the Show* on North Pier in 1954.

There were summer seasons at the Queen's Theatre in 1957 and 1958, as well as North Pier in 1961, and a brief appearance in a touring variety revue at the Grand in 1962. Indeed, Terry is pictured on the previous page at the Queen's in 1957 with fellow stars Vic Oliver, Jimmy Clitheroe and Anne Shelton. However, Terry cut back on live appearances following Lenny's success on children's TV and a lucrative contract advertising Trebor Mints.

Terry made TV appearances on *Blackpool Night Out* from the ABC in 1965 and 1967 and did a season of afternoon shows at South Pier in 1968. He died in 2008, aged 80.

# Keith Harris

**V**ENTRILOQUIST Keith Harris was back on TV in 2008 with sidekick Orville. Together they promoted foreign currency for the Post Office in a small-screen advertising campaign. The loveable green duck was instantly recognisable beneath brown paper and packaging as Keith attempted to save on air fare by sending his sidekick through the post.

And, it has to be said, many readers will no doubt also be able to make out Keith himself underneath all that hare – sorry, hair! – in the 1974 picture below. As a young 'vent', Keith, who hails from Poulton,

A young Keith Harris and friend in 1974.

Orville the Duck sets off in his new Mercedes, much to the surprise of Keith Harris, who has his own full-size Merc and an eye-catching number plate.

outside Blackpool, was about to start a summer season at the ABC Theatre, together with The Kaye Sisters, supporting camp comic Larry Grayson in *Grayson's Scandals*.

He was back at the ABC in 1977, by which time the buck-toothed rabbit had taken a back seat to Orville and a monkey with attitude called Cuddles.

In 1983 *The Keith Harris Show* was the Grand's summer entertainment, and five years later he joined Les Dawson and Frank

Carson at the Opera House, followed by no fewer than five seasons in *Keith and Orville's Magic Castle* at the Sandcastle.

In 1999 Keith became ringmaster in the Tower Circus and was back on stage at the Grand two years later for the season-long *Joe Longthorne Show*.

Keith Harris at the resort's Sandcastle Centre in 1990.

# Richard Hearne

CHILDREN'S TV comedy was in its infancy in the early fifties, but actor-acrobat-dancer Richard Hearne's madcap creation Mr Pastry can rightly claim to be its first star.

Mr Pastry tries his hand at golf at Knott End Golf Club in 1961.

Richard Hearne greets St Annes youngsters in 1961. He was appearing in the Opera House season show in Blackpool.

Mr Pastry was a big hit with kids and grown-ups with his walrus moustache, rimless specs, bowler hat and flapping coat-tails, and his slapstick antics and signature tune of *Pop Goes the Weasel*.

He visited Blackpool time and again to entertain locals, and each time he brought joy – and also brightened the lives of disabled children, helping raise funds for swimming pools for physically handicapped youngsters.

He told the *Gazette* he had raised £30,000 in four years, 'not a penny taken for expenses or administration, £30,000 raised, £30,000 has gone on the swimming pools'.

The comedian and comic actor had a score of comedy slapstick routines at his disposal, but was dogged throughout his career by the most successful – his one-man Lancers dance, which he performed during a successful season at Blackpool Opera House in 1961. He also appeared on the bill in Blackpool, at the Pavilion, the Palace and the Grand (in *Charley's Aunt*).

Multi-talented Hearne, who was originally a leading man in West End revues in the mid-1930s, also penned several thrillers which were performed on radio, and he dreamed of playing Hamlet. But, as Mr Pastry found out, there wasn't enough dough in Shakespeare...sorry, folks.

# Thora Hird

**T**HORA HIRD was a seaside landlady – no doubt complete with cruet set – in 1958. The comedy actress was performing in Gerald Savory's *Come Rain, Come Shine*, one of several comedies in which she had the audiences cheering for more at Blackpool's Grand Theatre.

Thora Hird with comedians Max and Syd Harrison in 1956.

Thora Hird with Mr and Mrs Tom Seed of the Crown Hotel, Corporation Street, Blackpool, in 1956.

Her first appearance was in 1953 when she was already well-known for her northern character cameos in British films as she teamed up with Arthur Askey for the summer play *The Love Match*.

Among other season runs was *Saturday Night at the Crown*, in 1956, when the *Gazette* reported of her role as gossip Ada Thorpe, 'In this sort of part, no-one can touch her – she is gloriously garrulous.'

*Happy Days* came in 1959, followed by *The Best Laid Schemes* in 1962 – in which she was again a seaside landlady, this time with a gift for hypnotism – and *My Perfect Husband* in 1965.

An OBE in 1983 was followed 10 years later by an even greater honour when she became a Dame at the age of 82, revisiting the Grand at that time for an ITV *South Bank Show* documentary, recalling her five season shows.

A devout Christian, Thora presented the BBC religious show *Praise Be!* for nearly two decades.

Thora, who also appeared in the long-running TV series *Last of the Summer Wine*, died in 2003, aged 91, in the actors' retirement home Brinsworth House in Twickenham.

Thora Hird presented a trophy to Mrs Eleanor Parkinson – owner of the best cared for stud of donkeys on Blackpool sands – in 1962.

# Stanley Holloway

THE PLAQUE marking the spot in Blackpool Tower where young Albert Ramsbottom was supposedly eaten by Wallace the lion in Stanley Holloway's monologue has long gone – just like the zoo and menagerie itself.

It was unveiled in 1978, 46 years on, by the man himself when his resort visit also included a command performance of the monologue for then mayor Margaret Riley in her Town Hall parlour.

The 88-year-old entertainer, who received a gold disc for worldwide sales in excess of two million, admitted that despite the strong Blackpool connections in the monologue, he had not actually appeared locally since the revue *Up and Doing* at the Grand Theatre in 1941.

Previous appearances had included the Grand in 1927 and several visits to the Palace between 1935 and 1940. He was also a star of the 1938 Opera House summer show.

Photographed shortly before he died in 1978 aged 88, Stanley Holloway visited Blackpool and unveiled a plaque at Blackpool Tower to commemorate his famous Lion and Albert monologue.

# Bob Hope

**C**OMEDY great Bob Hope not surprisingly packed houses on his three Blackpool appearances. Bob, born in South London but an American legend, performed two shows at the Opera House on Saturday 21 April 1951, when he also met his second cousin for the first time: Florence Biss, who lived in Cornwall Avenue, North Shore.

The *Gazette* reported: 'The moment he stepped on the stage and told the audience how thrilled he was at the wonderful weather he had brought with him, they were his friends. He revealed himself as a prince of patter and ace ad-libber, whose insouciant manner concealed the precision of a stopwatch and the polish of a chromium counter.'

After the shows, Bob met the Press at the Clifton Hotel and later went for a midnight stroll on the prom.

Bob Hope finds time to put his feet up before his Opera House show in 1951.

Autograph hunters rush foward as Bob Hope leaves the Clifton Hotel for the Opera House in 1951.

In an interview with a Chicago newspaper on his return to America, Bob described Blackpool as 'the English end of Coney Island, but instead of hot dogs and hamburgers, the sidewalk vendors sell delicacies called winkles, mussels and whelks. First I thought they were an English vaudeville act.'

The comedian had in fact entertained the troops with a visit to the United States Army Air Force base at Warton airfield in July 1943, and he made his last visit to Blackpool's Opera House on 28 October 1962, the final night of that season's Illuminations and the night before he appeared in London in the Royal Variety Show. Bob Hope died in July 2003, age 100.

# Rod Hull & Emu

**I**T WOULDN'T happen today, but this was the scene in Blackpool town centre in August 1981 when Rod Hull and his unpredictable Emu descended on an unsuspecting public to give them a taste of things to come at Christmas that year.

And what a surprise there was for Blackpool beauty queen Caroline Davies in her two-piece swimsuit, all ready and waiting for an un-politically-correct peck on the cheek.

Blackpool beauty queen Caroline Davies got quite a shock when she was set upon in Blackpool town centre by Emu.

Rod and the infamous television bird were busy promoting *Emu in Panto-land*, the first pantomime to be staged at the Grand Theatre for more than 30 years.

The troublesome twosome had previously performed in *The Good Old Days* season at the Winter Gardens Pavilion in 1972.

Rod, who was born in 1936, died tragically in 1999 when he fell off the roof of his house while adjusting a TV aerial.

Rod Hull and Emu take a look around from the roof of The Winter Gardens in 1972.

# Frank Ifield

**E**LEPHANTS have long memories, so perhaps this one greeted yodeller Frank Ifield, seen here in the ABC Theatre Bar, with the words of his Number One hit *I Remember You!*

The Coventry-born singer, who had spent 14 years in Australia, was headlining *Holiday Startime* in 1967. Also on the bill was an elephant called Tanya, a regular on TV.

Frank Ifield, star of the ABC *Holiday Startime* show in 1967, could hardly believe it when the barmaid turned out to be Tanya the elephant!

Frank Ifield and co-star Kathy Kirby at the ABC Theatre in 1964.

Animal rights protesters would have a field day today at the sight of baby Tanya perched on her front legs, rotating on a glitter ball. There was even a charity competition to guess her 'vital statistics', from the tip of her trunk to the end of her tail.

As a publicity stunt for the show, Tanya was pictured pulling a pint for Frank with a stick attached to the Watney's barrel. Also in the photograph are Tanya's owner Jenda Smaha and comedienne Audrey Jeans. Jimmy Tarbuck and the Barron Knights completed the show's line-up.

Frank had enjoyed his first ABC summer show three years earlier, from where he also starred in the first-ever *Blackpool Night Out* TV broadcast in 1964. He was in fine voice 20 years later when he played his third Blackpool season at the newly opened Sandcastle.

# Nat Jackley

**W**HO'S THIS with the strange expression, ill-fitting uniform and an outsized gun? It's the eccentric North-East comedian Nat Jackley, who chalked up an impressive seven Blackpool summer shows and made his home in St Annes.

Rubber-necked master of silly walks Nat Jackley, who starred in seven Blackpool summer shows.

A blast from the past for Nat Jackley at Gypsy Rosa Lee's Blackpool booth in 1982.

A master of silly walks and comic dances, Nat starred in variety, film and pantomime from the late 1940s to the mid-1980s.

With his trademark rubber-neck, skeletal frame and peculiar speech impediment, he was a formidable and funny pantomime dame. His first Blackpool appearance came in a touring production of *Jack and the Beanstalk*, which arrived at the Opera House in March 1945.

Two years later he was at the same theatre co-starring for summer with comedian Dave Morris in *Ev'ry Time You Laugh*. In 1948 Nat was back *for* two visits at the Palace in a West End touring revue, *Piccadilly Hayride*. Later the comic co-starred in the season show *Out Of This World* at the Opera House.

He also starred at the Queen's Theatre, formerly the old Feldman's, when it was reopened in 1953, and returned the following year. He appeared with Tessie O'Shea at the Hippodrome in 1956, the Queen's again in 1962 and Central Pier in 1970. He was also in the cast of the 1981 Royal performance at the Grand Theatre.

# Sid James

**S**ID JAMES was a much-loved face in British comedy – and what a face it was! The South African-born comedy actor was the star of countless *Carry On* movies and also appeared in summer shows

Sid James and Audrey Jeans took time off from *The Mating Season* for a visit to Blackpool Zoo in 1975.

Sid James filmed at the reins of one of Blackpool's famous landaus on the promenade in 1964.

and pantomime. Twice he was announced for seasons at Blackpool's Grand Theatre but heart scares prevented it, although he finally starred there with Beryl Mason in Sam Cree's farce *His Favourite Family* in 1969.

He returned to Blackpool in 1975, this time at the Winter Gardens, in *The Mating Season*, the year before Sid's tragic demise while on stage at the Sunderland Empire.

# Danny Kaye

'**G**OSH, this reminds me of the Houses of Parliament,' exclaimed Brooklyn-born Danny Kaye when he first saw Blackpool's Empress Ballroom, which he packed on 17 and 18 July 1952. Of Blackpool itself, he maintained, 'It's like me – it just isn't true.'

The *Gazette* reviewer said of his performance, 'Fundamentally it was a triumph of sheer personality which carried the house with it like a tidal wave. Danny took liberties with his audience that in a lesser performer would have spelled disaster. It was a virtuoso performance that fully merited the rapturous reception at the close.'

During the show Danny amazed onlookers by taking a break, sitting with his legs dangling over the edge of the stage, smoking a cigarette and chatting to the audience.

The entertainer, who died aged 74 in 1987, did not stay in the resort for those Fylde coast appearances, but got away from the hustle and bustle at the Hotel Majestic, along the seafront in St Annes.

Danny Kaye sits down on the job at the Empress Ballroom in 1952.

Danny Kaye at the Empress Ballroom in 1952.

# Laurel and Hardy

'**A**NOTHER fine mess you've gotten me into...' These are the world famous words delivered in so many black and white films by Laurel and Hardy, who appeared in Blackpool's *Palace Varieties* in June 1947.

Today, long after their deaths, these two geniuses of comedy probably have a greater following than at the height of their Hollywood stardom.

Their bill-topping appearance at the Palace was during the first of three British tours organised by Bernard Delfont after their film careers declined, and the two stars stayed at the Clifton Arms Hotel in Lytham. A *Gazette* reviewer said of their performance, 'You will laugh not so much at the words of the script as at the stars themselves who, in all their movements from the flick of Ollie's tie to the plaintive smile of Stan, suggest you are getting a four-dimensional view of their latest film.'

The comedy legends had previously visited Blackpool in August 1932 during a film promotion tour. After being met at Preston railway station they were driven in a four-car convoy through Lytham St Annes to the densely packed Blackpool promenade.

'Amazing,' said Stan, 'I had no idea Blackpool was such a wonderful place. I have never been to Blackpool before, though I always wanted to.'

Having arrived almost unnoticed during the day, they were mobbed by fellow guests at the Hotel Metropole and waved from a balcony as an estimated 100,000 crowd gathered. Later they attended a dinner in their honour at the Winter Gardens Baronial Hall. A visit to the Palace followed, where Laurel and Hardy briefly stepped on stage to joke with Arthur White.

Stan stayed up till 2am that morning as he was determined 'to have a quiet walk round Blackpool'. He managed to walk to the Pleasure Beach and back, and though the promenade was still packed with people, who hours earlier had been cheering him, not one recognised him.

The following day the comedians were still signing autographs until the last minutes as their train steamed out of Blackpool North Station for Manchester.

---

*Memories*

*'I was there in June 1947 when Laurel and Hardy tried to negotiate the steps down to the dressing room and Stan inadvertently tripped the portly Ollie. He turned and delivered his famous catchphrase about a fine mess and everybody roared with laughter.'*
*Neil Kendall, South Shore*

Oliver Hardy and Stan Laurel, who were mobbed in Blackpool in 1947.

# Joe Longthorne

JUST when there were fears that all the international names were missing out on summertime in Blackpool...along came Barry Manilow, Neil Diamond, Shirley Bassey and Judy Garland.

But instead of importing all the originals one at a time, they all appeared on one bill – courtesy of vocal impressionist Joe Longthorne.

Although Hull-born entertainer Joe turned professional in 1971, it was not until 1987 that he made his television breakthrough – as the special guest on the entire series of BBC TV's *Les Dennis's Laughter Show*.

That set him on the road to stardom and riches, as well as his own TV special and a return TV booking with Les for 1988.

Joe's love affair with Blackpool began with a first season at the North Pier in 1987, supported by Dana and Roy Walker, followed by a return two years later.

He helped set a box office record at the Opera House with *Superstars 93* alongside Little and Large, and while he said at the time he was coming to the end of his Blackpool summer season days, he vowed he would still be back in his favourite resort on a regular basis.

Lift off for Joe Longthorne from three of the Ray Cornell dancers ahead of his Seaside Spectacular on North Pier in 1987.

Joe Longthorne back home at the North Pier in 1997.

Joe Longthorne on stage at the Blackpool Grand Theatre in 2006.

True to his word he returned with a series of summer Sunday shows in 1994, a formula he repeated in 1996, and he was back for Blackpool North Pier summer seasons in 1997 and 1998.

Personal setbacks followed with a well-publicised health battle against leukaemia and a cash blow when in 2000 he was declared bankrupt with debts of more than £1 million, after once being one of Britain's highest-paid performers, with Rolls-Royces and Bentleys in the drive of his Berkshire home.

In the summer of 2004, still having treatment, the Blackpool favourite was forced to pull out of *The Joe Longthorne Spectacular* at the Opera House on doctor's orders. In 2005 he underwent a bone marrow transplant and happily made a successful stage comeback at the Grand Theatre in Easter 2006.

He has since toured extensively and starred at the Blackpool Pleasure Beach Paradise Room and the Grand in 2007. He renewed his commitment to North Pier with another summer season in 2008, when he declared, 'I love this theatre. Some of my happiest moments have been on this stage.'

# ✦ Johnny Mathis ✦

**A**H, TALK about wishing on a star...If ever a picture tells a story, just look at the star-struck expression on this young woman's face, as she meets the man on her album cover and gets his autograph.

The sultry-eyed sultan of croon Johnny Mathis clearly cast his spell over 18-year-old Lilian Riley, a hairdresser from Fleetwood, back in 1961, when she won a *Gazette* competition to meet her idol at the Hippodrome, Blackpool, where he was appearing in concert, backed by Ted Heath.

Her boyfriend Eric, according to our then entertainment reporter Michael Berry (who developed his own showbiz career as bubble-haired comedian and show host Lennie Bennett), watched nervously from a corner of the star's dressing room, but later agreed with his bedazzled girlfriend's verdict that Mathis was 'just wonderful'.

Starstruck – Lilian Riley with her idol Johnny Mathis, who appeared at the Hippodrome in 1961.

# Albert Modley

**T**HERE was a wealth of talent at the Royal Command Performance at Blackpool Opera House on 13 April 1955 in honour of the Queen and Prince Philip. Yet the biggest laugh was for veteran comic Albert Modley, walking on stage and bowing to the wrong side of the theatre. His jaw dropped when he saw the royal box was not there – and then he 'realised' it was on the opposite side, where he bowed, grinned and said in his Yorkshire accent, 'Flippin' 'eck, I thowt yer'd gone 'ome.'

His first Blackpool appearance was in 1932 in *Arcadian Follies* at South Pier, and in 1947 he was the star of Lawrence Wright's *On With The Show* at North Pier, where he also did two further seasons.

Central Pier runs for Peter Webster followed in 1953 and 1954 and, after several variety visits to the Palace in 1955 (the same year as his Opera House royal performance), he appeared there in the 1956 season show *Summer Showboat*.

Albert was back on Blackpool's Central Pier in 1962, stepping in for a sick Tommy Trinder, which led to headline billing there the following year – achieving a rare record of three shows at each of the resort's piers.

On arrival at Central Station, from London, Albert Modley, who had just finished a film with a horse-race sequence, could not resist a mount, so he borrowed Mick from a landau in May 1950.

# Morecambe and Wise

**B**RITAIN'S favourite double act Morecambe and Wise had a long-lasting love affair with Blackpool audiences spanning four decades.

Ernie saw the importance of the resort and once said, 'If you got a summer season in Blackpool, you reached the Mecca in showbusiness. It was a season of sheer joy.'

Fun on the Raikes Hotel bowling green for Morecambe and Wise, who were appearing at the North Pier in 1963.

Eric and Ernie spring a surprise on Valerie Barrett of Blackpool during a photocall for the *Morecambe and Wise Show* at the ABC Theatre in 1965.

Morecambe and Wise – originally known as Wiseman and Bartholomew – first appeared in Blackpool in the early 1940s, but had their comedy careers interrupted by World War Two. They were not seen back in the resort until April 1949, when they were billed second to a mind-reading act at Feldman's Theatre.

Their 43-year partnership and steady rise to stardom followed a heavy work schedule. Ernie recalled how in their heyday they 'crammed a summer season, pantomime, radio, variety tours and a television series into 52 weeks.'

In the 1950s they played four seasons in Blackpool, the first at the Winter Gardens Pavilion in 1953 in *Something to Sing About*. They then topped the bill at the Central Pier summer show in 1955, and again in 1957 and 1959.

Television had made Eric and Ernie the country's best-loved comedy duo by the time they returned to Blackpool to star in the North Pier's 1963 summer show. The show broke all box office receipt records for the previous 40 years. After this achievement the duo went to the US for television engagements. In 1965 they appeared at the ABC Theatre and made their last Blackpool appearance at the Opera House in October, 1976.

Comedy genius Eric collapsed and died, aged 58, after he had just finished a performance on stage in Tewkesbury in 1984.

Ernie – the one with the legendary 'short, fat, hairy legs' – made a career out of providing the laughs for Eric.

For four decades 'Little Ern' was on the receiving end of a comic genius and the butt of so many publicly-celebrated jokes, not least his 'toupée' of which Eric would often joke, 'You can't see the join.'

Ernie's last visit to Blackpool came in December 1992, for the filming of television documentary *Forty Minutes: The Importance of being Ernie*. He died in hospital, age 73, after heart trouble in 1999.

The double act will always be remembered for their fun-filled, frenetic Christmas TV specials. Their anthem *Bring me Sunshine* could not have been more appropriate for the duo, who lit up the lives of Blackpool holidaymakers.

Cricket fun for Morecambe and Wise at Stanley Park in 1957. They were starring in the Central Pier show *Let's Have Fun*.

# Robert Morley

**T**HE YOUNG lad with actor Robert Morley might have the look of comic Peter Kay, but he is actually Robert's son Sheridan, who was to find fame as a broadcaster. The picture was taken in the dressing room of Blackpool's Grand Theatre in 1956 when Robert – full name Robert Adolf Wilton Morley – was teamed up with stage and screen favourite Margaret Rutherford in Gerald Savory's comedy *A Likely Tale*.

Robert, who died in 1992, first played the Grand in September 1943 in Kaufman and Hart's *The Man Who Came To Dinner*, in which he played a pompous, overbearing drama critic called... Sheridan!

The following February he was back, this time in his own play *Staff Dance* with Beatrice Lillie.

*Hippo Dancing* was another Grand offering in February 1954, prior to a big success in London's West End, and three years later his play *Six Months Grace* brought his final Grand appearance.

Robert Morley and son Sheridan at the Grand Theatre in 1956.

# Anna Neagle

ANNA NEAGLE was the first showbusiness celebrity to switch on Blackpool Illuminations. In 1939, although the Illuminations were ready for staging, they were prevented by the start of World War Two. Restrictions on the use of fuel and decorative lighting and the austere climate of post-war Britain meant they did not come on again until 1949 – and stage and movie star Anna Neagle came to Blackpool to do the honours.

Anna appeared in three plays in the resort, starting in June 1944 at the Grand in a pre-London tour of Jane Austen's *Emma*, which the *Gazette* hailed as 'a personal triumph'.

She was back on the same stage in November 1959 in the comedy *The More the Merrier*. Her hat-trick of appearances was completed at the end of December 1963 at the Winter Gardens Pavilion in her first thriller, *Persons Unknown*.

However, she made *Gazette* headlines while visiting the resort for another reason in 1962, to watch the Blackpool Dance Festival. She had just set up a new dance studio venture and was pictured on the Promenade, opposite the Clifton Hotel, with her film producer husband Herbert Wilcox and another of the dance studio's directors, wartime heroine Odette Hallowes, who had worked as a British agent in France and was captured by the Gestapo.

Anna Neagle was swamped by the crowds as she arrived to switch on the 1949 Illuminations.

Anna Neagle takes a stroll along Blackpool promenade with her husband Herbert Wilcox and Odette Hallowes in June 1962.

Herbert told the *Gazette* that it was something of a sentimental journey because it had been at that hotel where he had first read the book *Odette* and decided to make a film of it, with Anna in the title role.

And Anna joined in: 'It was during the filming that the real Odette and I became friends – she is a wonderful person.'

Anna in her Blackpool dressing room in February 1965.

# Tessie O'Shea

EVEN celebrities fail to faze Blackpool's traffic wardens, as this picture, taken in 1968, goes to prove. Tessie O'Shea was greeted by a warden offering a friendly warning (rather than today's digital camera evidence and hard line ticket slapped on the windscreen) about her parking as she left a Clifton Hotel press

Tessie O'Shea is greeted by a traffic warden in 1968.

Tessie O'Shea and Ken Dodd exchange tickling sticks at a rehearsal for the *Big Show* at the Opera House, Blackpool, in 1968.

conference for Ken Dodd's Opera House season show in which she was the guest star.

Her trademark smile probably disguised her frustration, but if she had stayed in character from her previous Blackpool appearance, then Tessie would have had no problems dealing with anyone in officialdom.

Tessie O'Shea.

She was the formidable Ma Hornett in the comedy *Sailor Beware* at the Grand Theatre in 1958, and the *Gazette* reported, 'In full flight of fury her voice would render a regiment of sergeant majors powerless to make themselves heard.'

The Cardiff-born entertainer, affectionately known as Two Ton Tessie after the song written for her by Lawrence Wright, appeared in Blackpool over a span of 40 years, from variety at the Palace in 1933 to 12 summer shows, the first in 1934 and the last in 1972.

Tessie's 1930s summer show earnings from three seasons of North Pier's *On With The Show* and two seasons at Feldman's bought her a cottage in nearby Poulton.

After opening the Horseshoe Bar at the Pleasure Beach in 1963, Tessie went to work in America, appearing in Broadway musicals and Hollywood films including Disney's *Bedknobs and Broomsticks*. She later settled in Florida but frequently returned to Britain until her death in 1995.

# Wilfred Pickles

**H**IS long-running radio show was called *Have A Go*, and entertainer Wilfred Pickles did exactly that when he switched on Blackpool Illuminations in 1950. The show ran for 21 years from 1946 and always opened with the catchphrase, 'Ow do, are yer courtin'?'

Blackpool gave Wilfred his first variety show, the 1943 season offering *We're All In It*, at the Opera House, and in 1944, 1945 and 1947 he brought the popular *Have A Go* feature to the Palace Theatre.

In 1946 he came to the Grand Theatre in *Cure For Love*, also appearing for the 1951 season in *Hobson's Choice*, for one week each in 1952 and 1953 in *The Gay Dog*, and in 1957 in the play *Ride A Cock Horse*.

Wilfred Pickles switches on the Blackpool Illuminations in 1950.

Wilfred and his wife Mabel holidayed in nearby Lytham for more than 10 years. He said Lytham never changed: 'That's the beauty of it. It's natural and restful and we can get away from all the bustle of work.'

Halifax-born Wilfred also performed with his wife Mabel in the Royal Variety Performance at the Opera House in 1955.

Wilfred, who died in 1978, told the *Gazette* four years earlier: 'Blackpool is a happy town. As a boy I used to come here and I still think what I thought then, that Blackpool is a town run by magic.'

# Tyrone Power

'**A**S SOON as you see the tower, you know where you are immediately and geographically,' said American film star Tyrone Power as he looked out from his suite at the Imperial Hotel, Blackpool.

'Whoever built it had a grand idea', he added.

Dark, handsome and softly spoken, Power found international screen fame thanks to an 18-year association with movie giants 20th Century Fox, which began in 1936.

A smouldering heart-throb in the pre-war years, he came to Blackpool aged 43, to star in a production of Bernard Shaw's play *The Devil's Disciple* at the Grand Theatre in March 1956. Power played the part of Dick Dudgeon, last portrayed at the Grand Theatre by Robert Donat in 1940.

A *Gazette* reviewer said of his performance, 'He plays the young Dick Dudgeon with flash and fire. He speaks well and brings the animation of his film technique to a part that obviously requires it. He makes a handsome and likeable figure of the black sheep of the family, and inevitably he dominates the play.'

During his brief visit to the resort, Power requested a trip up the famous tower.

'I would like to see something of this place I have heard so much about,' he said as he left the hotel for a stroll along the promenade.

He also visited the Palace Cinema and sat in the centre of the front row of the circle – with fellow company members – for a private showing of one of his favourite films, in which he starred, *The Long Gray Line* (1954), a story of the United States Military Academy, West Point.

Little more than two years later – in November 1958 – Power died of a heart attack, aged 45, in Madrid after a duelling scene during the filming of *Solomon and Sheba*, in which he was starring alongside Gina Lollobrigida and George Sanders.

Tyrone Power took a stroll along the promenade during his Blackpool visit in 1956.

# Al Read

LANCASHIRE comedian Al Read followed a unique path to fame, which was to lead to six summer seasons in Blackpool. The 41-year-old highly successful boss of a family pie-making business was spending his evenings as an after-dinner speaker, poking fun at everyday characters, when his talent was first spotted by a radio producer.

From this, building on the observational styles and techniques of earlier comics such as Billy Russell and Robb Wilton, he gradually evolved his somewhat deadpan, yet instantly recognisable, stage persona. His caricatures of northern life tickled the nation in the fifties and sixties. Among his classics were the wife in the kitchen, the know-all johnny, the car park attendant and the man trying to get into the football match.

Al Read with W.C. Heard at a St Annes YMCA garden party in 1951.

Master monologist Al Read made his home in St Annes.

Using no props or costumes, the master monologist cleverly honed anecdotes and ideas into tightly-structured, fast-paced routines. In an instant, audiences could readily identify with the many absurdities of life he skilfully placed before them.

Read soon found himself with his own long-running radio series, *Such Is Life*. A successful season at Blackpool Central Pier in 1951 followed and the road to stardom saw him top of the bill at the London Palladium. He was also one of the stars of the first-ever Royal Command Performance outside London, at the Blackpool Opera House in 1955. His most popular catchphrases, 'You'll Be Lucky' and 'Right Monkey', also became the titles of two successful revues staged at London's Adelphi Theatre in 1954 and 1956.

For many years Read famously lived in nearby St Annes. Here, his often ostentatious choice of cars and noted sartorial elegance made him a familiar sight. He and his wife Joyce were great friends with fellow showbusiness stars George and Beryl Formby, who also lived in St Annes, and together they became stalwart supporters of the amateur dramatic scene on the Fylde Coast.

In 1960, having sold the family business, Read moved, albeit somewhat belatedly, into television. Here, for ITV, he first fronted *Life and Al Read*, later moving on to *Al Read Says What A Life*.

Al Read steps out of his chartered light aircraft at Squires Gate after a trip to York Races in 1964. With him are singers Marlane Marcel and Dick Francis from the Central Pier show.

Unquestionably the last of the great radio comedians, Al Read's shows regularly attracted an audience in excess of 35 million. When in 1976 the BBC discovered that they had wiped all the tapes of his classic shows, he happily returned to the studios to re-enact the routines. In 1985, two years before his death, in typical style, he published a charmingly modest autobiography entitled *It's All In The Book*. He died at his home in the Yorkshire Dales in 1987, aged 78.

*Memories*

'I was a boyhood pal of Al's second son Alex. I can recall Al taking the business of being funny very seriously and obsessing with every detail. I remember visiting his home when he had bought suitcases in the same colour as his newly acquired Rolls-Royce – and then agonised over whether his fans might think it too over the top.'
*Richard Fulford-Brown, Lytham*

'I remember vividly going to see a panto in Liverpool which starred Al Read. Mum was a Londoner and had difficulty understanding the Lancashire accent. I used to have to interpret for her. During the interval mum turned to the lady sitting next to her and said, "He's not much good is he?" referring to Al. "That is my husband!" came the tart reply. Mum turned a delicate shade of puce!'
*D. Condon, Watson Road, Blackpool*

# Paul Robeson

**T**HE POLITICALLY controversial actor and bass singer Paul Robeson brought pleasure to millions. Blackpool was one of the first towns Robeson played in this country on his first trip across the Atlantic during the 1920s.

Blackpool Odeon manager Rupert Todd presents Paul Robeson with a giant stick of Blackpool rock following his performance in September 1958.

He was in the cast of *Voodoo*, a play set in Africa, at the Opera House in September 1922.

Then, following his success in the Drury Lane production of *Show Boat*, Paul returned to Blackpool's Opera House in June 1929 and again in July 1931.

Three years later Paul was at Feldman's Theatre and then back at the Opera House in 1936 and again on Palm Sunday 1949 when the *Gazette* reported he was 'gay and grave, sombre and humorous' in a concert that included a speech from *Othello*.

Soon after, Paul's passport was withdrawn following a controversial visit to the Soviet Union.

When the ban was lifted in 1958 he undertook a European tour, making his final Blackpool appearance at the Odeon on 21 September, where he was presented with a giant stick of rock by manager Rupert Todd (pictured with him on the previous page).

Paul congratulated his audience on living in a town which was 'the centre of the country's culture during the summer.'

He died in Philadelphia, aged 77, in January 1976, after spending the final decade of his life in silence and bitter seclusion.

*Memories*

'I was reminded of a 1959 school trip from St Kentigern's to Stratford Memorial Theatre to see *Othello*. Paul Robeson was Othello, Mary Une was Desdemona and Sam Wanamaker was Iago. Also in the cast list as soldiers, citizens and officers were Albert Finney, Roy Dotrice, Ian Holm, Diana Rigg and Vanessa Redgrave. I didn't realise I was watching actors who would become household names.'

*Pauline Wilkinson, Marton, Blackpool*

# Lily Savage

**T**HESE days Scouse entertainer Paul O'Grady is very much part of the mainstream with his own award-winning teatime TV chat show. But turn the frock, sorry, clock back 20 years and Paul's alter ego, drag creation Lily Savage – the self-styled 'blonde bombsite from Birkenhead' – was a mainstay of Blackpool's gay scene.

O'Grady's support of the fledgling Flamingo nightspot in the 1980s is well-documented and owner Basil Newby recalled that after performing in drag Paul would even help to clean the then Talbot Road club in the early hours when the punters had gone.

His ever-growing following around the country led to national fame on the small screen with Lily hosting BBC's *Blankety Blank* – a role once filled by the late Fylde funnyman Les Dawson.

Unlike the busty dames with acres of padding, Paul's visual appearance depended on his own slim build and height, as can be seen in the leopardskin patterned creation he wore in 1996 promoting *The Lily Savage Show* at North Pier. His summer run was followed by a Christmas show at the Opera House.

Lily Savage tries her hand at the wurlitzer on North Pier in 1996.

Paul O'Grady, alias Lily Savage, tried hard to get into the festive spirit for his 'Christmas Cracker' show at the Blackpool Winter Gardens in 1996.

# Harry Secombe

**H**ARRY Secombe was a megastar when he blazed into Blackpool to take top billing in a summer season at the Palace Theatre in 1960. A household name by that time, Secombe hadn't forgotten the kindness of Blackpool in the early days of his showbiz career.

Secombe said, 'In the depths of my heart I have a very warm spot for Blackpool. It was the first variety spot I played, after the Windmill Theatre, at the beginning of my career. And come to think of it – the money wasn't bad.'

Harry Secombe at a Lytham St Annes Bathing Beauty competition judge in 1951.

Keen photographer Harry brought one of his eight cameras to Blackpool for his 1960 summer season.

In return, Blackpool had a warm spot for the Goon with the golden voice.

Demobilised in 1946, Secombe appeared at the Windmill Theatre, where he provided a comic turn in between girly shows. Although he had appeared on television and radio with *Variety Bandbox*, he soon found himself reduced to second-spot comedian touring the provinces.

His first spot here, also at the Palace, was in 1950, when he received a standing ovation. The *Gazette* reviewer of the time, commenting on his unique comedy style, said, 'Harry can take it that Blackpool completely approves of his madness.'

In 1951 he was back in Blackpool in a show called *Happy Go Lucky* at the Opera House, the same year that saw the start of the *Goon Show* on radio – he had to get up at the crack of dawn on Sunday to make the drive from Blackpool to London for recordings – and his first *Royal Variety Show* appearance.

Loved by millions for his pioneering comedy brilliance, Harry returned to the resort in the 1960 season with *Secombe Here*, scripted by Jeremy Lloyd and Jimmy Grafton and co-starring Harry Worth and Ruby Murray.

Harry rented a house in Poulton as a family home during the season. He was accompanied by his wife Myra and children Jennifer and Andrew.

Arriving with luggage at Blackpool Airport for rehearsals with Dickie Henderson at North Pier in 1967.

Golf was a passion of Harry's, and 'there will be a welcome in the bunkers' was the ominous inscription on a golf token presented to him by the Variety Golf Society, who played weekly competitions at St Annes Old Links throughout the 1960 season. Society captain was Bruce Forsyth, and among his fellow players were Glenn Melvyn, Toni Dalli and Jimmy Lee.

Two decades later Harry was back on the Fylde coast for a concert at Fleetwood's Marine Hall, and in 1996 he chatted with Ken Dodd on North Pier as part of a *Songs of Praise* programme.

With his powerful tenor voice, Sir Harry – who was knighted in 1981 – also found acclaim in the musicals *Pickwick* and *Oliver* and he topped several Opera House Sunday concerts from 1967 to 1973. He retired from showbusiness in 1999 after a lifetime of comedy, song and charity work.

The Prince Of Wales led tributes to a comic genius when Sir Harry Secombe died from cancer at the age of 79 in April 2001.

# Tommy Steele

TOMMY Steele was back in Blackpool at the Grand Theatre in 2008 in the title role of musical comedy *Doctor Dolittle*. However, back in 1957, when Tommy first came to Blackpool for a month of afternoon shows at the old Palace Theatre, nobody could accuse him of doing little!

That was the year when the Cockney's big hits *Singing The Blues*, *Butterfingers* and *Water Water* were all top of the hit parade and later re-entered the charts.

One headline-grabbing episode came when Tommy, staying at the old Majestic Hotel, St Annes, was asked to leave when he woke everyone up by playing the drums in the hotel ballroom at 3am.

His previous Blackpool appearances include topping the bill in *The Big Show* of 1960 at the Opera House with Alma Cogan.

He was back 10 years later in *The Tommy Steele Show* at the ABC with Welsh songthrush Mary Hopkin, returning to the same theatre in 1979 for his all-singing, all-dancing *An Evening With Tommy Steele* summer run.

*Doctor Dolittle* star Tommy Steele pictured outside Blackpool Grand Theatre in 2008.

In 1986 he played eight successive Sundays at the Opera House with his West End song and dance show.

His 2008 Grand return gave him the remarkable record of 51 years between bill-topping performances.

Tommy Steele in Blackpool in 1957.

Tommy Steele rehearsing in 1957.

*Memories*

'My own memory of Tommy Steele was of playing against him at Stanley Park. I was working back-stage at the Queen's Theatre in the year that Tommy was top of the bill at the Opera House in 1960. The Queen's challenged the Opera House to a game of football, and Tommy showed he was a decent player on the wing. Also playing was Italian tenor Toni Dalli, but the best of the showbiz footballers was 'Our Eli', Eli Woods, from the Jimmy James act. The final result – Opera House 4, Queen's 2. We were always going to struggle, though, as diminutive Jimmy Clitheroe would insist on going in goal for us! Happy days!'
Barry Stott, Thornton Cleveleys

Tommy Steele takes the umpire's chair at South Shore Tennis Club in 1960 with fellow show stars Bruce Forsyth, Glenn Melvyn, Harry Secombe and Toni Dalli.

# Jack Storey

**L**ANCASHIRE comedian Jack Storey used his experiences as a Blackpool hotelier – his guesthouse was called Storeyville – in a camp seaside patter act.

A name in variety, Jack went on to star in several summer shows, such as North Pier in 1953, 1954, 1964 and 1965, the Hippodrome in 1958 and Central Pier in 1967.

He was proposed as a Liberal candidate for Blackpool's Bispham Ward, but did not stand due to his showbusiness commitments, which included touring the country as a dame in pantomime. He died in 1982 at the age of 69.

Comedian and Blackpool hotelier Jack Storey in 1962.

*Memories*

'*When I was a boy, back in the fifties and sixties, my parents, regularly took us to stay at Jack Storey's hotel, Storeyville. There was never a dull moment, with his hawkish charm and one-line quips, entertaining on stage and off. His hotel was adorned with souvenirs and signed photos of stage and screen stars, national and international. Piped music from the forties would always be heard. Clearly a well connected man and true comedian of a bygone era. A piece of magic and fond memories!*'

*Roger Burton*

Jack Storey and Anne Shelton, who appeared together in *On With The Show* on the North Pier in 1954.

*Jack Storey gave me my first showbiz break as a drummer in 1963 in the old St Annes Pier Theatre. A great character, remembered always with a smile, and his catch phrase, "well, ya do, don't ya."'*

*Pete Lindup, Warley Road, North Shore*

# ✦✧✦ Jimmy Tarbuck ✦✧✦

**F**ORMER holiday camp entertainer Jimmy Tarbuck made his Blackpool debut in a week of cabaret at the Sands Club, Marton, in 1963, returning the following year as one of five stars in the North Pier summer show.

Likely lad from Liverpool…Jimmy Tarbuck was in Blackpool in 1967 to share top-billing at the ABC with Frank Ifield.

Jimmy Tarbuck signs autographs for young fans.

The Liverpool comic had broken into the big time as compère of ITV's *Sunday Night At The London Palladium* and maintained a TV career with a busy round of live performances.

In 1967 he enjoyed top billing at the ABC with Frank Ifield and shared the honours there with Kenneth McKellar in 1971.

There were Sunday appearances at the Opera House during the late 1970s and 80s – often with his golfing pal Kenny Lynch on the same bill – and the two of them came back in 1995 to provide the Christmas cabaret at the newly opened Pleasure Beach Paradise Room.

# Tommy Trinder

**T**HE TILTED pork pie hat was a trademark for Cockney comic Tommy Trinder, but when he was in Blackpool he could also be found sucking on a stick of seaside rock.

Before the 1960s Tommy had appeared in the resort just once, in 1948, in a week of variety at the Palace Theatre.

Then in 1961, after many appearances on TV's *Sunday Night At The London Palladium*, he was signed up for Central Pier to top the bill in the annual *Let's Have Fun* summer show.

He was so well received that Tommy was back the next year with the show, renamed *You Lucky People* to cash in on his catchphrase.

In 1965 he completed a hat-trick of Blackpool season shows and was the star of *Show Time* on North Pier.

Comedian Tommy Trinder started off a charity mile of coins on Blackpool seafront in August 1965 – the dogs obviously thought there were treats in store!

Tommy Trinder enjoys a stick of Blackpool rock during the 1961 summer season.

# Max Wall

**M**ASTER of the funny walk was the unmistakeable Max Wall, whose star creation Professor Wallofski was actually 'born' in Blackpool.

A comedy genius, Wall first made his name as a dancer and matured into a stand-up comedian and fluent mime, starring in the 1930 *Royal Variety Show* at the London Palladium.

In the company of Maurice Chevalier and Mistinguet, he played throughout Europe and took his act to the United States.

In 1941, serving in the RAF under his real name, Maxwell Lorimer, he was posted to Blackpool and billeted in Handsworth Road, North Shore.

Shows included the 1941 pantomime *Robinson Crusoe* at the Opera House, a Cole Porter musical at the Grand and the 1945 summer show *Hoopla* at the Grand.

During his Blackpool war years, Max is said to have devised his mad-cap professor routine to entertain fellow RAF trainees at the old Jubilee Theatre inside the Co-operative building in Coronation Street.

The reaction was so positive that an alter ego was born, complete with grotesque flowing wig and black tights, which would come to dominate the British variety circuit. He shared top billing at the Palace in 1951 and returned two years later for a revue alongside Julie Andrews.

He became the highest-paid performer on radio and television and one of the first tax exiles, living in Jersey, but – and how times change! – as his first marriage crumbled, and he was pictured in a tabloid with a comely beauty queen, he fell from grace and was shunned by the BBC. He plummeted from West End bill-topper to professional wilderness.

The slog back in the sixties came via the northern working men's club circuit. He became a favourite at the Jack of Diamonds, at the old Empire cinema in Marton. His fortunes were further revived in later life with some superb straight acting in theatre, TV and cinema.

His private life was more fraught. Thrice married, he died, something of a recluse, alone in a one-room council bedsit in 1990, aged 81.

Master of the funny walk, Professor Wallofski, the creation of Max Wall, pictured in 1975.

# Marti Webb

**R**EADERS will not need such a long *Memory* to recall when Marti Webb performed the show's biggest song of that name in *Cats*. It was in 1989 that Marti brought her West End role of Grizabella the glamour cat to Blackpool's Opera House in the first provincial season of Andrew Lloyd Webber's record-breaking musical.

But Marti's first resort appearance had been almost three decades earlier at the Grand Theatre, when she had a supporting role in the farce *Pillar to Post* starring Glenn Melvyn, Danny Ross and Betty Driver in 1960.

Marti was back at the Grand five years after that in another comedy, *My Perfect Husband*, in which she played the girlfriend of Thora Hird and Freddie Frinton's son – the last time in her career that she did not have a singing role.

In 1993 Marti opened the show for Michael Barrymore during a four-week season at the Opera House, and in June 1996 she was Eva Peron, star of *Evita*, at the Grand.

That same theatre hosted *Magic of the Musicals* in 1999, not once but twice, with the second visit starring Marti, who had been forced to pull out of the original concert through illness. Her last Blackpool appearance was again in *Magic* in 2002.

Marti Webb in *Cats* at Blackpool Opera House in 1989.

# ⋆⋆⋆✶ Gary Wilmot ✶⋆⋆⋆

**T**ODAY he is best known for his roles in musical theatre, but when Gary Wilmot made his first big impression on Blackpool audiences it was as a comedy entertainer.

His solo act, which saw him mimic popular names of the day, proved to be the real highlight of the game show *Come On Down* when it was the 1985 summer season attraction at the Grand Theatre.

Two years later he was back at the Grand in the fast revue *Gary Wilmot and Co.*, returning to the resort – to acclaim – in 1996 for a pre-Christmas season of *Me and My Girl*.

This West End revival of the 1930s comedy ended its provincial tour with a month at the Opera House.

Hats off to Blackpool from Gary Wilmot, who starred in Me and My Girl in 1996.

# Barbara Windsor

**A**S EASTENDERS' pub landlady Peggy Mitchell, Barbara Windsor is more likely to have a plate of jellied eels in her hand. But back in 1992, long before the BBC TV soap beckoned, bubbly Barbara Windsor could be seen on Blackpool sea front whetting her appetite with oysters. She was starring on North Pier with Bernard Bresslaw in the season show *What A Carry On*.

Yet when the *Gazette* caught up with her outside Robert's Oyster Bar, she did not see much of a funny side to Blackpool Promenade.

'There is just too much tat. Everywhere you look along this stretch there is bankrupt stock and the like being sold from little stalls. Even the Golden Mile does not hold the same magic it used to,' she claimed off-camera, during filming for BBC's *The Travel Show*.

Barbara, evacuated to the resort during World War Two, did not share her concerns to viewing millions on screen, claiming, 'Blackpool is still a wonderful place for me.'

Her previous summer run had been in 1981, at the Grand with Trevor Bannister and Jack Smethurst in the farce *The Mating Game*.

Barbara Windsor outside the famous Robert's Oyster Bar on Blackpool Promenade in 1992.

Barbara Windsor on the carousel on North Pier in 1992.

# Mark Wynter

**W**HY WAS Mark Wynter looking so glum when the *Gazette* took this photograph of him on the dodgems at Central Pier in 1966? According to the caption, the car was the only type he was going to be allowed to drive during his Blackpool summer season on the pier, having lost his licence for speeding.

He revealed, 'It happened two weeks ago in Rutland. I've already sold my car and taken up running. I run everywhere – it's probably good for you!'

Born Terence Lewis, the singer and actor made his name on TV pop shows in the late 1950s and his concert appearances in Blackpool included the Hippodrome and no fewer than 20 visits in Harold Fielding's legendary Sunday shows at the Opera House. His summer shows were the ABC in 1965, with Morecambe and Wise, and 1966 on Central Pier with Winifred Atwell and Eddie Calvert.

Turning his talents to musicals and plays, Mark appeared at the Grand Theatre in the comedy thriller *The Ghost Train* in April 1985, starred in Ken Hill's musical version of *The Phantom of the Opera* in November 2000 and was back two years later as Daddy Warbucks in *Annie* with Su Pollard. His most recent visit was in the Agatha Christie murder mystery *Spider's Web* at the Grand Theatre in 2009.

Pop star Mark Wynter looking glum on a Blackpool dodgem in 1966.

Mark Wynter and fellow star of *South Pacific* Jessica Martin officially open the Grand Theatre's new Matcham Court canopy in 1997.

# OPERA HOUSE STARS

## Roll of Honour

1889 Wilson Barrett
1890 Brinsley Sheridan
1891 Osmond Tearle
1892 Charles Wyndham
1893 Kate Vaughan
1894 C. Aubrey Smith
1895 Emma Hutchison
1896 Weedon Grossmith
1897 Agnes Hewitt
1898 Marie Studholme
1899 Ada Blanche
1900 Ada Reeve
1901 Lillie Langtry
1902 Julia Neilson
1903 Amy McNeil
1904 Charles Chaplin
1905 Victor Andre

1906 Ellaline Terriss
1907 Albert Chevalier
1908 James Forbes-Robertson
1909 Percy Hutchison
1910 Annie Huges
1911 Evelyn Millard
1912 Anna Pavlova
1913 Fred Terry
1914 Edward Compton
1915 Cicely Courtneidge
1916 Neil Maskelyne
1917 Seymour Hicks
1918 Sir Thomas Beecham
1919 Robertson Hare
1920 Phyliss Neilson-Terry
1921 Frank Forbes-Robertson
1922 Mrs Patrick Campbell

1923 Bransby Williams
1924 Edna Best
1925 Raymond Huntley
1926 Jessie Matthews
1927 Evelyn Laye
1928 Wilfred Hyde-White
1929 Peggy Ashcroft
1930 Sir John Barbirolli
1931 Gracie Fields
1932 Carl Brisson
1933 George Clarke
1934 Billy Bennett
1935 Albert Burdon
1936 Randolph Sutton
1937 Fred Sanborn
1938 Stanley Holloway
1939 George Formby
1940 Arthur Askey
1941 Frank Randle
1942 Webster Booth & Anne Ziegler
1943 Wilfred Pickles
1944 Sid Field
1945 Jimmy Jewel & Ben Warriss
1946 Josef Locke
1947 Dave Morris
1948 Charlie Chester
1949 Arthur Haynes
1950 Nat Jackley
1951 Vera Lynn
1952 Terry Thomas
1953 Harry Secombe
1954 Tony Hancock
1955 Alma Cogan
1956 Eve Boswell
1957 Yana
1958 David Whitfield
1959 Jill Day
1960 Tommy Steele
1961 Shirley Bassey
1962 Eddie Calvert

1963 Jimmy Edwards
1964 Rosemary Squires
1965 Stan Stennett
1966 The Bluebell Girls
1967 Bruce Forsyth
1968 Tessie O'Shea
1969 Val Doonican
1970 The Bachelors
1971 Rudy Horn
1972 Cilla Black
1973 Danny La Rue
1974 Norman Vaughan
1975 Freddie Starr
1976 Don Maclean
1977 Dawson Chance
1978 Tom O'Connor
1979 Frank Carson
1980 Mike Yarwood
1981 Ken Dodd
1982 Syd Little & Eddie Large
1983 Paul Daniels
1984 Ruth Madoc
1985 Tommy Cannon & Bobby Ball

Aled Jones joins the Opera House roll of honour in 1995.

Darren Day's name joins the long list of stars at the Opera House.

1986 Grace Kennedy
1987 The Nolans
1988 Les Dawson
1989 Marti Webb
1990 Dana
1991 42nd Street
1992 Paul Nicholas
1993 Joe Longthorne
1994 Michael Barrymore
1995 Aled Jones
1996 Darren Day
1997 Kid Creole

1998 Darren Day
1999 Russ Abbot
1999 Shane Richie
2000 Lesley Joseph
2001 Lord of the Dance
2002 Whistle Down The Wind
2003 Cats
2004 Joe Longthorne
2005 David Essex
2006 Bradley Walsh
2007 Roy 'Chubby' Brown
2008 Jane McDonald

# THE GRAND THEATRE

## Star Appearances

1894 Wilson Barratt
1895 Cissie Loftus
1896 Marie Studholme
1901 Dan Leno
1902 Lillie Langtry
1903 Ellen Terry
1905 Sarah Bernhardt
1906 Herbert Beerbohm Tree
1908 Seymour Hicks
1909 Ellaline Terriss
1915 Matheson Lang
1923 Jack Hulbert
      Evelyn Laye
1929 Gracie Fields
1933 Marie Tempest
1934 Douglas Fairbanks Jr
1935 John Mills
1936 Sybil Thorndike
      Yvonne Arnaud
1937 Leslie Henson
1938 Stewart Granger
      Gladys Cooper
1939 Jessie Matthews
      Glynis Johns
      Rex Harrison
      Peggy Ashcroft

The Grand Theatre.

1940 John Le Mesurier
      Tessie O'Shea
      James Mason
      Robert Donat
      Alec Guinness
      George Cole
1941 Stanley Holloway
      John Gielgud
      Vivien Leigh
      Cyril Cusack
1942 Bobby Howes
      Harry Korris
      Edith Evans
      Noel Coward
1943 Richard Tauber
      Googie Withers
      Richard Attenborough
      Robert Morley
1944 Peter Cushing

Jack Hulbert.

Coral Browne
Anna Neagle
Wilson, Kepple and Betty
John Clements
Kay Hammond
1945 Richard Greene
Cecil Parker
Max Wall -
Rob Wilton
Joan Greenwood
1946 Wilfred Hyde-White
Dulcie Gray
Ian Carmichael
1947 Irene Handl
Wendy Hiller
Jack Buchanan
1948 Peter Ustinov
Denholm Elliott
Ted Ray
Gertrude Lawrence
Michael Redgrave
1949 Jean Simmons
Margaret Lockwood
Norman Wisdom
Donald Peers
Fay Compton
1950 Kenneth Moore
Josef Locke
1951 Jack Smethurst
Leslie Phillips
Donald Sinden
Robertson Hare

Peter Sallis
1952 Sam Wanamaker
Wilfred Pickles
Margaret Rutherford
Geraldine McEwan
Joss Ackland
1953 Ralph Richardson
Michael Denison
Arthur Askey
Emlyn Williams
1954 Virginia McKenna
Roger Moore
Diana Wynward
Peter Byrne
Dandy Nichols
Fenella Fielding
1955 Geoffrey Palmer
Flora Robson
Paul Schofield
Glen Melvyn/Danny Ross
Donald Wolfit
Andrew Sachs
1956 Sylvia Sims
Ian Holm
Tyrone Power
Anton Rodgers
Hattie Jacques
Thora Hird
1957 Trevor Bannister
Ronnie Corbett
Donald Pleasance
Moira Shearer
Barbara Murray
1958 Vanessa Redgrave
Lynn Fontanne
Arthur Lowe
Jack Hulbert
George Formby
Cicely Courtneidge
1959 Leslie Crowther
Pat Phoenix
1960 Wendy Craig
Michael Bentine
Clive Dunn
Dick Emery
Pat Kirkwood
Alistair Sim
1961 Kenneth Williams
Sheila Hancock
Beryl Reid
Betty Driver
Timothy West
1962 Jimmy Logan

Ted Ray.

Dora Bryan.

|      |                   |
|------|-------------------|
|      | Trevor Howard     |
|      | Alfred Marks      |
|      | Peggy Mount       |
|      | John Barrie       |
| 1963 | Moira Lister      |
|      | Dora Bryan        |
|      | Jimmy Clitheroe   |
|      | Susannah York     |
| 1964 | Michael Crawford  |
|      | Hylda Baker       |
|      | John Barron       |
|      | Richard Briers    |
| 1965 | Harry H. Corbett  |
|      | Amanda Barrie     |
|      | Freddie Frinton   |
| 1966 | John Hanson       |
| 1967 | Ron Moody         |
|      | Nicholas Parsons  |
| 1968 | Helen Shapiro     |
|      | Jack Douglas      |
| 1969 | Veronica Lake     |
|      | John Inman        |
|      | Sid James         |
| 1970 | Jimmy Jewel       |
| 1971 | Bill Kenwright    |
|      | David Jason       |
| 1981 | Petula Clark      |
|      | Bob Monkhouse     |
|      | Barbara Windsor   |
|      | Jack Smethurst    |
|      | Roy Castle        |
|      | Simon Williams    |

|      |                   |
|------|-------------------|
|      | Jess Conrad       |
|      | Roy Barraclough   |
| 1982 | Robin Askwith     |
|      | Simon Ward        |
|      | Bernie Winters    |
|      | Mandy Rice-Davies |
|      | Larry Grayson     |
|      | Prunella Scales   |
|      | Rula Lenska       |
|      | Lennie Bennett    |
|      | Frank Thornton    |
| 1983 | Derek Batey       |
|      | Max Boyce         |
|      | Jeremy Beadle     |
|      | Cleo Laine        |
|      | The Spinners      |
|      | Vera Lynn         |
|      | Stan Boardman     |
| 1984 | Brian Murphy      |
|      | Nigel Kennedy     |
|      | Kevin Whately     |
|      | Roy Kinnear       |
|      | Richard Madeley   |
|      | Norman Collier    |
|      | Freddie Starr     |
|      | Jim Bowen         |
|      | Les Dawson        |
|      | Keith Chegwin     |
|      | Charlie Williams  |
|      | Barbara Dickson   |
| 1985 | Anthony Quayle    |
|      | Su Pollard        |
|      | Acker Bilk        |
|      | Showaddywaddy     |

Jimmy Jewel.

Larry Grayson.

Keith Barron
The Flying Pickets
Michael Barrymore
1986 Bobby Crush
Wayne Sleep
Ruth Madoc
Eric Sykes
Christopher Biggins
1987 Tony Britton
Ruthie Henshall
Liz Fraser
Gary Wilmot
Danny La Rue
Norman Wisdom
1988 Kate O'Mara
Lorraine Chase
The Beverley Sisters
Frankie Vaughn
Linda Lusardi
Julian Lloyd Webber
Geoffrey Hughes
1989 Ross Kemp
Paula Wilcox
Courtney Pine
Bruce Forsyth
Des O' Connor
The Grumbleweeds
Brian Conley
The Nolans
Alvin Stardust
1990 Roy Marsden
David Griffin
Hale and Pace
Richard Digance
Mollie Sugden

Little and Large
Kathy Staff
1991 Caroline Quentin
Pam Ferris
Frank Windsor
Reginald Marsh
1992 Freddie and the
Dreamers
Bobby Davro
The Krankies
Bernard Cribbins
Jules Holland
Eddie Izzard
1993 Susan Penhaligon
Angela Thorne
The Hollies
Billy Pearce
Melanie B
Robert Powell
1994 Adam Faith
Midge Ure
Labi Siffre
Millicent Martin
Bonnie Langford
Liza Tarbuck
Duncan Norvelle
Patrick Mower
June Brown
Frank Skinner
Stefan Dennis
Val Doonican

Norman Collier.

Patrick Mower.

1995 Mark Curry
David Tennant
Richard Wilson
John Alderton
Hinge & Brackett
Jack Dee
1996 Andrew O'Connor
David Jacobs
Marti Webb
The Drifters
Sheila Ferguson
Lorna Luft
Willie Rushton
1997 Tony Robinson
Christopher Timothy
John Mortimer
Gemma Craven
Jean Fergusson
George Melly
Shirley Anne Field
Julian Clary
1998 Honor Blackman
Ned Sherrin
Ken Morley
Jason Donovan
Jasper Carrott
Rodney Bewes
Henry McGee
Joe Pasquale

Stephen Tompkinson
Frank Finlay
1999 Paul Nicholas
Peter Bowles
Errol Brown
Michael Elphick
Phil Cool
Tim Brook-Taylor
Frank Carson
The Stranglers
Richard Stillgoe
2000 Humphrey Littleton
Sam Kane
Darren Day
David Haig
Ian Lavender
Brian Cant
Jimmy Cricket
George Sewell
Mark Wynter
Johnnie Casson
2001 Victor Spinetti
Gordon Kaye
Ardal O'Hanlon
Stephanie Beacham
Jimmy Tarbuck
Bill Bailey
Robert Powell
Adam Rickitt

Robert Powell.

Ricky Tomlinson.

2002  Vince Hill
David Soul
Diana Quick
Jonathan Morris
Ann Charleston
The Barron Knights
Gerry & The Pacemakers
Vicki Michelle
Barry Cryer
The Stylistics

2003  Gwen Taylor
Toyah Wilcox
Uri Geller
Matthew Kelly
Colin Baker
The Chuckle Brothers
Gillian Taylforth
Jeffrey Holland

2004  Fred Dibnah
Gyles Brandreth
Frazer Hines
Judy Cornwell
Elkie Brooks
Cannon & Ball
Jimmy Osmond
Linda Nolan
Derek Acorah

2005  Gareth Hunt
Tony Hadley & Martin Fry
Graham Seed
Ray Alan and Lord Charles
Dave Willetts
Aled Jones
Kenny Baker

2006  Derren Brown
Ricky Tomlinson
Joe Longthorne

Julia Watson
Alexandra Bastedo
Max Bygraves
Jack Ryder

2007  Lenny Henry
Bernie Nolan
Shobna Gulati
Derren Nesbitt
Richard Blackwood
Alfie Boe

2008  Sandra Dickinson
Tommy Steele
Leslie Grantham
Simon MacCorkindale
Michael Praed
Joe McGann
Steven Houghton
Claire Sweeney
Jason Manford
James Alexandrou
Joe Brown

2009  Neil Stacy
Denis Lill
Basil Brush
Tim Flavin
Samantha Barks

Su Pollard and Claire Sweeney.

# BLACKPOOL ILLUMINATIONS

## ✦ Switch~on Stars ✦

1934 Lord Derby
1935 Audrey Mossom
1936 Sir Josiah Stamp
1937 Duke of Kent
1938 Coun Mrs Quayle
1939 Cancelled – War Years
1949 Anna Neagle
1950 Wilfred Pickles
1951 Stanley Mathews
1952 Valerie Hobson
1953 George Formby
1954 Gilbert Harding
1955 Jacob Malik
1956 Reginald Dixon
1957 John H. Whitney
1958 A.E. 'Matty' Matthews

1959 Jane Mansfield
1960 Janet Munro
1961 Violet Carson
1962 Shirley Ann Field
1963 Cliff Michelmore
1964 Gracie Fields
1965 David Tomlinson
1966 Ken Dodd
1967 Dr Horace King
1968 Sir Matt Busby
1969 Canberra Bomber
1970 Tony Blackburn
1971 Cast of TV's *Dad's Army*
1972 Danny La Rue
1973 Gordon Banks
1974 Wendy Craig

Blackpool Pleasure Beach and the Illuminations.

The Bee Gees turn on the Illuminations in 1995.

1975 Tom Baker
1976 Miss UK Carol Ann Grant
1977 Red Rum
1978 Terry Wogan
1979 Kermit the Frog and the
Muppets
1980 Cannon and Ball
1981 Earl and Countess Spencer
1982 Rear Admiral
'Sandy' Woodward
1983 The Coronation Street Cast
1984 Johannes Rau and David
Waddington, MP
1985 Joanna Lumley
1986 Les Dawson
1987 BBC *Holiday* presenters
Frank Bough, Ann Gregg
and Kathy Tayler
1988 Andrew Lloyd Webber and
Sarah Brightman
1989 Frank Bruno

1990 Julie Goodyear and Roy
Barraclough
1991 Derek Jameson and Judith
Chalmers
1992 Lisa Stansfield
1993 Status Quo
1994 Shirley Bassey
1995 Bee Gees
1996 Eternal
1997 Michael Ball
1998 Chris De Burgh
1999 Gary Barlow
2000 Westlife
2001 Steps
2002 Ronan Keating
2003 Blue
2004 Geri Halliwell
2005 Chris Evans
2006 Dale Winton
2007 David Tennant
2008 The Stig, *Top Gear*

# Roll of Honour

Donald Armstrong
Kirk Atkinson
Phil Baker
John Baxter
Peter Benson
Elizabeth Beswick
Geoff Billington
Donald Boon
Lonen Booth
Chris Boyes
Melvin Brandon
Michael Bridge
Derek Brown
James Cecil Brown
Johnnie Casson
Fred & Angela Champion
Peter Collinson
Michael Conradd
Bill Cropper
David & Carole Cyster
Emily Dickson
Hannah Dickson
Craig David Dunn
Elsie Eastwood
George Eaves
Victoria Eaves
Rita Elliott
Alan Ellis
Joan Ellis
Mr Howard Fleming
Jennie Isabel & Ian Gammon
Gregor Gillespie – Goodnight Productions
Nellie Gray
Renée Greenwood
Yvonne Gregitis
Peter Griffin
Peter S Hardman
Alfred Hawcroft

James Haselup
Edward Hey
Raymond Hibberd
Harold Hodgson
Kathleen Hughes
Stanley Hull
Slim Ingram
James Jackson
Peter & Tina Kenniford
Derek King (Bronco Billy)
Frank Kirby
Kathleen Knott
Colin Edwin Macleod
Joyce & Ted McMinn
Jonathan McNicholl
Barry McQueen
John James Massey
Ronald Mattock
Alan Mullin
Rebecca Anne Fleming Neal
Gordon Oates
Bob Perry
William C Platt
Jacqueline Victoria Pratt
Francis Price
Philip J Private
Ronald Russell
Elsie Sadek
Margaret A Sanderson
Sam & Sylvia Sanderson
Mark Singleton
Joan Smith
Keith Studd
Patrick Tommany
Beryl Toon
Barrie Townsley
Carol Williams
Vera Wiseman